Twentieth Century
DESIGN

Twentieth Century
DESIGN

A DECADE-BY-DECADE EXPLORATION OF GRAPHIC STYLE

Tony Seddon

PRINT

20TH CENTURY DESIGN.

Manufactured in China.

Conceived, designed, and produced by
Quid Publishing
Level 4 Sheridan House
114 Western Road
Hove BN3 1DD
www.quidpublishing.com

For more excellent books and resources for designers, visit www.MyDesignShop.com.

18 17 16 15 14 5 4 3 2 1

ISBN-13: 978-1-4403-3617-1

Distributed in Canada by Fraser Direct
100 Armstrong Avenue
Georgetown, Ontario, Canada L7G 5S4
Tel: (905) 877-4411

Contents

Introduction

Above *At a glance, the cover of the first issue of* Blast *could be fronting a punk fanzine from 1976—even the name of the publication sounds right. However, it was actually published by painter Wyndham Lewis in 1914.* Blast *aimed to drive out the visual conservatism of the Victorian era by encouraging the adoption of modern graphic styles.*

As is the case with many publishing projects that I've been involved in over the years, the idea for *Twentieth Century Design* evolved from a conversation. James Evans of Quid Publishing noted that discussions during development meetings would occasionally turn up the idea that a book design might benefit from "a 1950s retro look" and realized that the term was being used in a generic sense to describe any number of historical graphic design styles. What is a true 1950s look, as opposed to a 1930s or 1940s look? This book aims to address that question.

It may seem at times, particularly in the pages covering the early third of the twentieth century, that the text switches from a narrative about graphic design to one about art. In reality, art and graphic design are inextricably mixed and, certainly before the advent of the modern graphic design industry, graphic design was created almost exclusively by artists. Before Morris Fuller Benton coined the phrase graphic design in 1922, designers were known as commercial artists. It's clear that graphic designers who think a little like artists are often the ones that create the groundbreaking work that goes on to influence their contemporaries, so in that sense "graphic design" style is evolving today just as it did a hundred years ago.

The *Blast* cover shown on the left is a good example of how difficult and indeed surprising it can be to accurately place a piece of graphic design in a particular decade. The bold typography set at a sharp angle on the bright magenta paper stock could have appeared on the cover of a punk fanzine from the late 1970s. However, *Blast* was a short-lived literary magazine (only two editions were produced) written primarily by the English painter Wyndham Lewis in 1914. It's interesting to note that *Blast* was conceived as a riposte to the overbearing influence of the Italian Futurist Filippo Marinetti, and as a vehicle to promote Vorticism, the British take on Futurism. In this sense the rebellious intentions of the magazine are similar in nature to the punk fanzines, so there is a visual connection spanning the sixty or so years between Vorticism and Punk. The designers and writers behind the work were aiming at very similar targets.

As you progress through the book you will come across the profiles of thirty influential graphic designers—three per decade. Don't be surprised if a profile appears in a decade you wouldn't expect. Most of the designers profiled enjoyed, or are still enjoying, careers spanning more than one decade, so I have placed them where I feel they produced some of their most significant and influential work, or where their personal style fits with a particular movement, visual trend, or technological breakthrough.

Creating this book has proved to be a very enlightening experience; it's easy to discount how extraordinarily influential the graphic design styles of the last century were and of course still are today and, rather like fashion styles, how often elements of one style are retained by another. I hope you discover as much inspiration in the following pages to inform your own sense of design style as I did while writing the book.

Tony Seddon, 2014.

The Merrill C. Berman collection

Merrill C. Berman's collection of twentieth-century graphic design and typography is best known for its strengths in Russian Constructivism, Bauhaus, and Dada—styles which are now recognized as integral to the broader history of avant-garde artistic production. Berman began collecting political memorabilia as a boy and rekindled his interests in early American political posters, textiles, ferrotypes, and buttons in the 70s. This shift led him toward graphic material and, while researching the resurfacing Art Deco and Art Nouveau posters of Mucha, Cassandre, and Privat-Livemont, Berman was introduced to Russian photomontage and political posters. He turned his focus toward the avant-garde and these acquisitions,

along with an immensely significant 1929 work by Herbert Bayer, *Section Allemande*, provided the foundation for the collection. Berman continues to broaden his collection, which includes works by the most influential graphic designers of the twentieth century— Bayer, A. M. Cassandre, E. McKnight Kauffer, and Alexander Rodchenko, to name a few. He invites scholarly research on his collection, participates in numerous museum exhibitions to make the work accessible to the larger public, and has been extremely helpful during the production of this book.

A selection of images from the collection can be viewed online at *mcbcollection.com*, and any used in this book are indicated by a credit line that appears beneath the caption.

Above Section Allemande *by Herbert Bayer, 1930.*
Collection Merrill C. Berman

1900–1909

The time span for each movement indicates the style's accepted period of popularity; styles generally continued to be referenced for a time after the dates indicated here.

Arts and Crafts 1860–1910

Art Nouveau 1890–1914

Vienna Secession 1897–1932

● Peter Behrens designs *Feste des Lebens und der Kunst: Eine Betrachtung des Theaters als höchsten Kultursymbols* (Celebration of Life and Art: A Consideration of the Theater as the Highest Symbol of a Culture). It is thought to be the first instance of sans-serif type used as running text in a book layout.

● The Vienna Secession establishes its style with posters by Koloman Moser and Alfred Roller for the 13th, 14th, and 16th group exhibitions.

● The *Doves Press Bible*, designed by Edward Johnston, is published by T. J. Cobden-Sanderson and Emery Walker at the Doves Press.

● The Vienna Secession's experimental magazine *Ver Sacrum* (Sacred Spring) ceases publication.

● Koloman Moser and Josef Hoffmann form the Wiener Werkstätte (Vienna Workshops) to produce high-quality furniture and printed matter.

● Will Bradley is appointed art director for American Typefounders and publishes *The American Chap Book*.

00   01   02   03   04

Plakatstil (Sachplakat) 1905–1930

Futurism 1909–1930

● Lucian Bernhard enters a design contest and creates his poster for Priester matches, thus establishing the *Plakatstil* style.

● Peter Behrens designs a fully coordinated brand for AEG (Allgemeine Elektrizitäts-Gesellschaft), considered to be the first example of a corporate identity system.

● Peter Behrens and Lucian Bernhard co-found the Deutscher Werkbund (German Association of Craftsmen).

● Frank Pick is appointed Director of Publicity at London Underground.

● Morris Fuller Benton designs News Gothic for American Type Founders.

● Filippo Marinetti publishes his *Manifesto of Futurism*.

*News Gothic

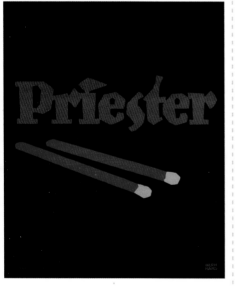

05   06   07   08   09

1910–1919

World War One begins

Art Nouveau 1890–1914

Vienna Secession 1897–1932

Plakatstil (Sachplakat) 1905–1930

Futurism 1909–1930

● Peter Behrens designs his poster for AEG Lamps.

● Will Bradley is appointed art director of *Good Housekeeping*, *Century*, and *Metropolitan* magazines.

● Lucian Bernhard designs Bernhard Antiqua.

● The *Wonderground* map is designed for London Underground by Max Gill, Eric Gill's younger brother.

● Filippo Marinetti publishes his Futurist poem *Zang Tumb Tumb*.

● Wyndham Lewis publishes *Blast* magazine.

● Saville Lumley designs his poster *Daddy, what did YOU do in the Great War?*

● Alfred Leete designs his poster *Britons [Lord Kitchener] wants YOU*.

Daddy, what did _YOU_ do in the Great War?

10   11   12   13   14

Bernhard Antiqua

Dada 1916–1932

De Stijl 1917–1931

Bauhaus 1919–1933

● Elbert Hubbard of the Roycroft Press is drowned in the sinking of the RMS *Lusitania*.

● Frederick Spear designs his poster *Enlist* in the wake of the sinking of the RMS *Lusitania* by a German U-Boat.

● The London Underground roundel is designed by Edward Johnston.

● The Hungarian literary magazine *Ma* (Today) is edited by Lajos Kassák.

● Marcel Duchamp creates his Dada sculpture *Fountain* from a urinal.

● James Montgomery Flagg designs his poster *I Want YOU*, the U.S. equivalent of *Britons* [*Lord Kitchener*] *wants YOU*.

● Hans Rudi Erdt designs his poster *U-Boote Heraus!* (U-Boats Out!).

● Julius Klinger designs his poster *8. Kriegsanleihe* (8th War Loan).

● El Lissitzky designs his poster *Beat the Whites with the Red Wedge*.

● Edward McKnight Kauffer designs his poster *Soaring to Success! Daily Herald—the Early Bird*.

● The Bauhaus opens its doors in Weimar for the first time.

● El Lissitzky develops PROUN (Project for the Affirmation of the New).

15   16   17   18   19   ▷

1920–1929

● The term "Constructivism" is coined by Vladimir Tatlin and Alexander Rodchenko.

● The Stenberg brothers produce their first movie poster for the film *The Eyes of Love*.

Vienna Secession 1897–1932

Plakatstil (Sachplakat) 1905–1930

Futurism 1909–1930

Dada 1916–1932

De Stijl 1917–1931

Bauhaus 1919–1933

Constructivism 1921–1934

● Alexander Rodchenko is appointed Director of the Museum Bureau and Purchasing Fund in Russia.

● Herbert Bayer begins his studies at the Bauhaus.

● William Addison Dwiggins coins the phrase "graphic design."

● Oskar Schlemmer designs the Bauhaus seal.

● Joost Schmidt designs his poster for the Bauhaus exhibition.

● Alexander Rodchenko and Vladimir Mayakovsky produce *Novyi LEF* (Left Front of the Arts) magazine.

● A. M. Cassandre designs his *Au Bucheron* poster.

● Kurt Schwitters publishes *Merz*.

● Alexander Rodchenko designs his famous *Knigi* (Books) poster featuring a portrait of Lilya Brik.

● El Lissitzky publishes *The Isms of Art*.

20   21   22   23   24

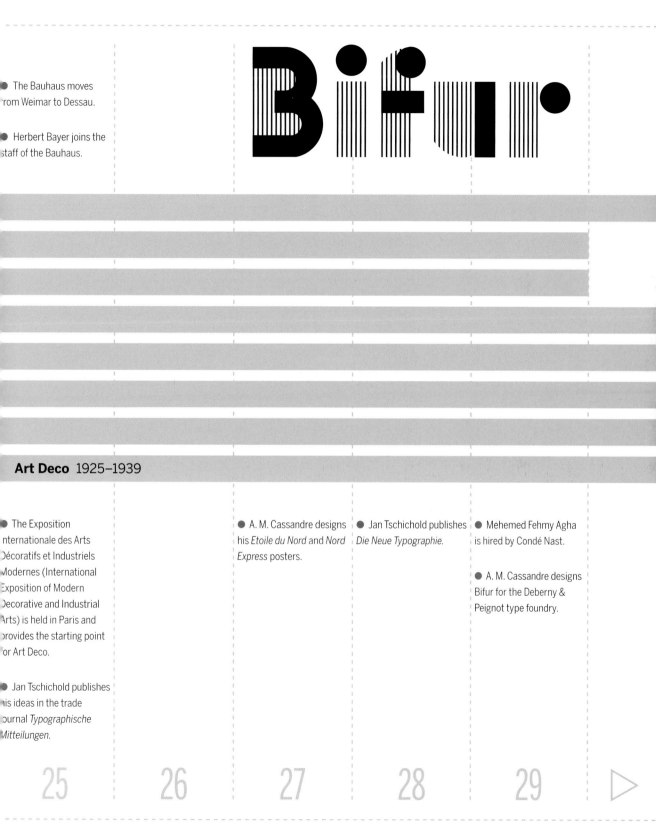

● The Bauhaus moves from Weimar to Dessau.

● Herbert Bayer joins the staff of the Bauhaus.

Art Deco 1925–1939

● The Exposition internationale des Arts Décoratifs et Industriels Modernes (International Exposition of Modern Decorative and Industrial Arts) is held in Paris and provides the starting point for Art Deco.

● Jan Tschichold publishes his ideas in the trade journal *Typographische Mitteilungen.*

● A. M. Cassandre designs his *Etoile du Nord* and *Nord Express* posters.

● Jan Tschichold publishes *Die Neue Typographie.*

● Mehemed Fehmy Agha is hired by Condé Nast.

● A. M. Cassandre designs Bifur for the Deberny & Peignot type foundry.

25   26   27   28   29   ▷

1930–1939

- A. M. Cassandre designs his *L'Atlantique* poster.

Vienna Secession 1897–1932

- Cipe Pineles is hired by Mehemed Fehmy Agha and joins the staff at Condé Nast.

- Henry Beck designs his famous map for London Underground.

- Socialist Realism replaces Constructivism as the official graphic design style of the Soviet Union.

Dada 1916–1932

- A. M. Cassandre designs his first advertisements for Dubonnet.

- The Bauhaus closes.

De Stijl 1917–1931

Bauhaus 1919–1933

Constructivism 1921–1934

Art Deco 1925–1939

Mid-century Modern 1933–1960

- Alexey Brodovitch is appointed art director at *Harper's Bazaar*.

- Studio Boggeri, specializing in poster design, is founded in Milan, Italy,

30 31 32 33 34

● Lester Beall begins work on his poster series for the Rural Electrification Administration.

● The Nazis stage their Degenerate Art exhibition in Munich.

● The new Bauhaus is established in Chicago.

● Herbert Bayer moves to the U.S. from Germany.

World War Two begins

● Herbert Matter receives his first commission from the Swiss National Tourist Office.

● A. M. Cassandre designs his *Normandie* poster.

● Herbert Matter relocates to the U.S.

● Ludwig Hohlwein begins work on a series of propaganda posters for the Nazi government.

● A. M. Cassandre designs Peignot for the Deberny & Peignot type foundry.

PEIGNOT

35   36   37   38   39

● Alvin Lustig receives his first book-cover commission from publisher New Directions.

● Rosie the Riveter makes an appearance on J. Howard Miller's poster *We Can Do It!*.

● Alvin Lustig designs *Staff*, an in-house publication for *Look* magazine from 1944-45.

Mid-century Modern 1933–1960

● Jean Carlu designs his poster *America's Answer! Production*.

● Cipe Pineles is appointed art director of *Glamour* magazine, the first woman ever to hold the position for a major publication.

● Mehemed Fehmy Agha retires as art director at Condé Nast.

40   41   42   43   44

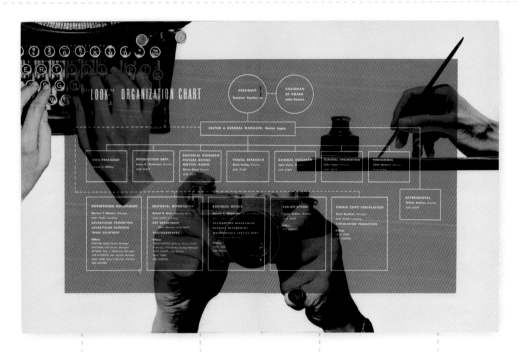

● Paul Rand writes and designs his book *Thoughts on Design*.

● Max Huber designs the first of a number of posters for the Autodromo Nazionale Monza (National Racetrack of Monza.)

● The New Bauhaus closes after it is absorbed by the Illinois Institute of Technology.

International Typographic Style 1945–1980

● *Design Quarterly*, the Walker Arts Center's magazine, is first published.

● Jan Tschichold joins Penguin Books.

● Jackson Burke designs Trade Gothic just before joining Linotype as director of type development.

● The advertising agency Doyle Dane Bernbach (DDB) opens for business on Madison Avenue, New York City, and goes on to create numerous memorable campaigns including the VW *Think Small* series.

Trade Gothic

45   46   47   48   49

1950–1959

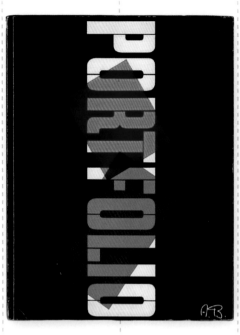

● Josef Müller-Brockmann begins work on a series of road safety posters for the Swiss Automobile Club.

● Alexey Brodovitch designs the first of only three issues of *Portfolio* magazine.

● Josef Müller-Brockmann begins work on a series of concert posters for Zurich Town Hall.

● Saul Bass designs his first title sequence for the movie *Carmen Jones*, directed by Otto Preminger.

Mid-century Modern 1933–1960

International Typographic Style 1945–1980

● Push Pin Studios is formed in New York City.

50   51   52   53   54

IBM

● Paul Rand designs the IBM logo.

● Adrian Frutiger designs Univers.

● Saul Bass designs the promotional posters and the title sequence for Otto Preminger's *The Man with the Golden Arm*.

● Max Miedinger and Eduard Hoffmann design Neue Haas, later to be renamed Helvetica.

● Seymour Chwast and Milton Glaser become the sole partners in Push Pin Studios.

Pop Art 1957–1972

Helvetica

55   56   57   58   59   ▷

1960–1969

● The *First Things First Manifesto* is written by British designer Ken Garland and is signed by himself and 21 other designers and illustrators. The manifesto is subsequently updated and republished in 1999.

● The term "Op Art" is first used in an article in *Time* magazine.

● Letraset dry transfer lettering is launched.

International Typographic Style 1945–1980

Pop Art 1957–1972

Sabon

● Herb Lubalin forms Herb Lubalin Inc.

● Jan Tschichold designs Sabon.

60   61   62   63   64

● The "Big Five" of Psychedelia, Rick Griffin, Alton Kelley, Victor Moscoso, Stanley Miller (better known as Stanley Mouse), and Wes Wilson, design numerous concert posters, notably for Bill Graham at the Fillmore Auditorium.

● Milton Glaser designs the iconic *Dylan* poster— over 6 million copies are subsequently sold.

● Andy Warhol designs the album cover for the Velvet Underground's *Andy Warhol*.

● Peter Blake and Jann Howarth design the album cover of *Sgt. Pepper's Lonely Hearts Club Band* by The Beatles.

● Saul Bass wins an Oscar for his documentary *Why Man Creates*.

● Herb Lubalin designs *Avant Garde* magazine.

● Lance Wyman designs the logo and signage system for the Olympic Games in Mexico.

Psychedelia 1965–1972

Op Art 1965–1970

● Storm Thorgerson and Aubrey Powell form Hipgnosis.

65   66   67   68   69

1970–1979

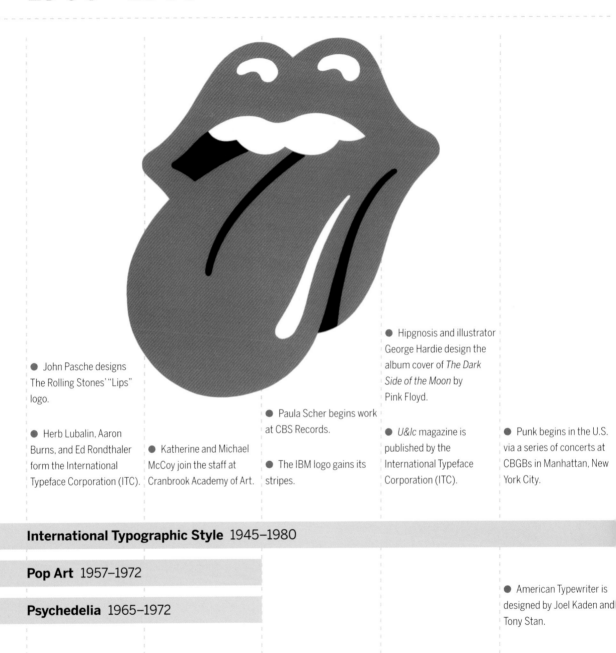

● John Pasche designs The Rolling Stones' "Lips" logo.

● Herb Lubalin, Aaron Burns, and Ed Rondthaler form the International Typeface Corporation (ITC).

● Katherine and Michael McCoy join the staff at Cranbrook Academy of Art.

● Paula Scher begins work at CBS Records.

● The IBM logo gains its stripes.

● Hipgnosis and illustrator George Hardie design the album cover of *The Dark Side of the Moon* by Pink Floyd.

● *U&lc* magazine is published by the International Typeface Corporation (ITC).

● Punk begins in the U.S. via a series of concerts at CBGBs in Manhattan, New York City.

International Typographic Style 1945–1980

Pop Art 1957–1972

Psychedelia 1965–1972

● American Typewriter is designed by Joel Kaden and Tony Stan.

American Typewriter

70 71 72 73 74

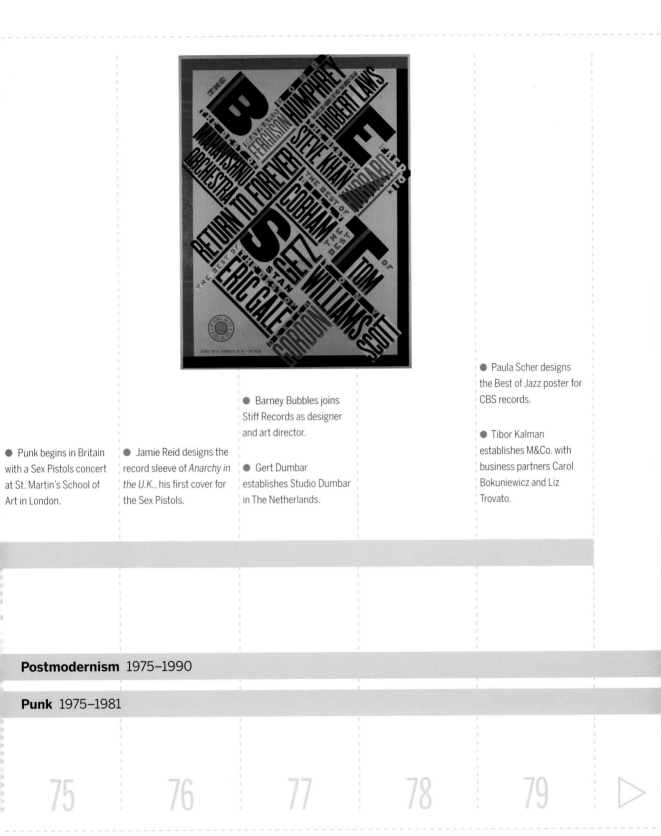

● Paula Scher designs the Best of Jazz poster for CBS records.

● Tibor Kalman establishes M&Co. with business partners Carol Bokuniewicz and Liz Trovato.

● Barney Bubbles joins Stiff Records as designer and art director.

● Punk begins in Britain with a Sex Pistols concert at St. Martin's School of Art in London.

● Jamie Reid designs the record sleeve of *Anarchy in the U.K.*, his first cover for the Sex Pistols.

● Gert Dumbar establishes Studio Dumbar in The Netherlands.

Postmodernism 1975–1990

Punk 1975–1981

75 76 77 78 79 ▷

1980–1989

THE FACE No. 42 ● OCTOBER 1983 75p

THE FACE
BODY AND SOUL

THE HIDDEN FACE OF FANTASY SEX
IN THE MIX: SEARCHING FOR N.Y'S PERFECT BEAT
EXCLUSIVE: INSIDE FIORUCCI'S PRIVATE MUSEUM

ANNIE LENNOX UNMASKED · JAMIE REID · BRIAN ENO
GWEN GUTHRIE · MEL GIBSON · CUSTOM SCOOTERS

● *The Face* magazine launches in London.

● *ID* magazine launches in London.

● Erik Spiekermann establishes MetaDesign in Berlin, Germany.

● Neville Brody is appointed art director of *The Face*.

● PostScript is created by John Warnock, Charles Geschke, Doug Brotz, Ed Taft, and Bill Paxton, providing one of the principal building blocks for the desktop publishing revolution.

● The Apple Macintosh computer is announced with the *1984* ad spot directed by Ridley Scott and screened during the a break in the third quarter of Super Bowl XVIII.

● The first set of icons for the Mac are developed by Susan Kare and Bill Adkinson

● Rudy VanderLans, Zuzana Licko, Marc Susan, and Menno Meyjes found *Emigre* magazine.

Postmodernism 1975–1990

Punk 1975–1981

80   81   82   83   84

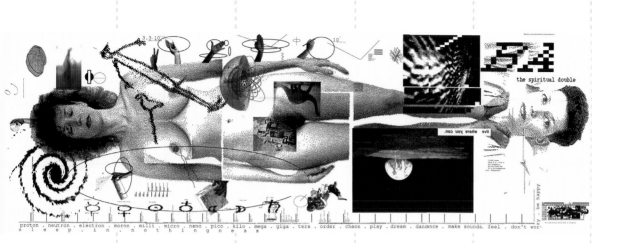

proton . neutron . electron . moron . milli . micro . nano . pico . kilo . mega . giga . tera . order . chaos . play . dream . dancance . make sounds. feel . don't wor-
s l e e p . i n . n o t h i n g n e s s

TRAJAN

- *HOW* magazine begins publication.

- *MacWorld* and *MacUser* magazines both begin publication.

- Aldus launches PageMaker, the first desktop publishing application designed to create layouts.

- Aldus founder Paul Brainerd coins the phrase "desktop publishing."

- Neville Brody is appointed art director of *Arena*.

- April Greiman uses the new digital technology to design issue #133 of *Design Quarterly* as a fold-out poster.

- Adobe launch their first version of vector graphic drawing software Illustrator.

- Quark Inc. launch page layout software QuarkXPress.

- Neville Brody 10-year retrospective is held at the Victoria and Albert Museum in London.

- Carol Twombly designs Trajan, one of the earliest typefaces designed for Adobe that never existed as a hot metal font.

- David Carson designs and art directs *Beach Culture* magazine and launches Grunge style.

The Digital Age 1985 to present day

85   86   87   88   89   ▷

1990–1999

- Tibor Kalman is appointed design director of *Interview* magazine.

- FontShop International is launched by Neville Brody and Erik Spiekermann.

- Adobe launches their first version of image editing software Photoshop.

- Tibor Kalman becomes editor-in-chief of Benetton's *Colors* magazine after creating the initial design proposals a year earlier.

- David Carson designs and art directs *Ray Gun* magazine.

- Adobe introduces layers to Photoshop, providing an enormous leap in creative flexibility for designers and illustrators.

The Digital Age 1985 to present day

90   91   92   93   94

what if..?
e se..?

Mrs Eaves

● Paula Scher begins work on posters and promotional material for The Public Theatre in New York City.

● Mrs Eaves is designed by Zuzana Licko of Emigre.

● Stefan Sagmeister designs the cover for Lou Reed's album *Set The Twilight Reeling*.

● David Carson designs travel magazine *Blue*.

● Apple launch their "Think Different" ad campaign.

● Adobe launch the first version of their page layout software InDesign.

● The *First Things First Manifesto 2000* is published.

95   96   97   98   99

1900s

The early years of the twentieth century were, for some, still firmly rooted in the preceding nineteenth. Class division continued to dominate society on both sides of the Atlantic and, while the moderately rich were celebrating the promise of a new century of technological wonder and opportunity, the lives of ordinary working people remained largely unchanged. Nonetheless, societal development rarely stood still from the 1900s onward, especially in terms of the domestic lifestyle of the majority of citizens in the developed world.

Technological advances introduced new products to the market, and this increase in manufacturing called for a larger workforce. More people relocated to towns and cities in search of this industrialized form of work and, as a result, improved infrastructures were needed for transportation and housing. The arrival of motion pictures also changed the way many people viewed the world; in urban areas electric lighting and a host of domestic appliances became more commonplace; powered flight became a reality; and by 1909 Henry Ford's Model T hinted at an age where everyman could aspire to own an automobile.

For graphic designers (or "commercial artists" as they were then known), these developments and the accompanying consumer-driven retail opportunities presented a potentially rich source of work, but it was not just demand that drove the changes. Advances in print technology, paper manufacturing, and specialist finishing machinery meant mass communication via printed media increased in volume on a previously unprecedented scale. As we will see while we progress through the next ten decades, graphic style seldom chose to rest on its laurels. Nevertheless, at the beginning of the twentieth century two important movements originating from the mid to late 1800s continued to prevail: Arts and Crafts, and Art Nouveau.

The legacy of nineteenth-century style

At the turn of the century, both Arts and Crafts, and Art Nouveau (called *Jugendstil* in Germany) continued to exert their influence on artists and designers until other newer avant-garde graphic styles falling under the umbrella of Modernism began to dominate.

William Morris, the English-born all-rounder and principal advocate for the Arts and Crafts movement, established the Kelmscott Press in 1891 to publish books in limited editions using hand-set type and woodcut illustrations. Morris was not keen on the mechanization of typesetting and printing, and, in line with the movement's specific rejection of machine-production techniques, he felt that the new hot-metal Linotype machines removed the element of craft from the typesetting process. The Kelmscott Press produced over fifty superbly crafted titles in its day and was a success despite the fact that, as a private press, it was never intended to be run as a commercial venture geared to mass production. Morris believed good design made art more accessible to the working classes, but ironically only well-off patrons could afford to purchase Kelmscott editions. This fact, which shares a degree of commonality with the Arts and Crafts movement in general, should not detract from the important contribution the Kelmscott Press made to the development of graphic design, and there is a positive commercial aspect of Morris's legacy. His rigid principles and experiences helped successive generations of designers recognize the need to strive to retain high standards of design quality and integrity while adapting to an industrialized environment in order to produce high-quality products that could retail at lower prices.

The distinctive style of Kelmscott editions was widely referenced,

Above *Alphonse Mucha is known as one of the most prolific protagonists of Art Nouveau style and produced many advertising posters, including this 1898 example for Job cigarette papers.*

Left *This rather sinister 1901 poster was designed by German illustrator Thomas Theodor Heine to promote a political cabaret in Munich. Heine was well known for his work for the satirical magazine Simplicissimus.*
Collection Merrill C. Berman

most notably by the somewhat more commercial operation known as the Roycroft Press set up by Elbert Hubbard in East Aurora, New York. Indeed, Hubbard was accused of outright imitation by many detractors although in truth he opened up the style to the general public by making his products more affordable. In England, the Doves Press was established by T. J. Cobden-Sanderson and Emery Walker and in 1903 they published the *Doves Press Bible*, a beautiful five-volume piece which included initials designed by the renowned calligrapher Edward Johnston (see pages 50 and 57).

Above *A page from the* Doves Press Bible, *T. J. Cobden-Sanderson and Emery Walker, 1903.*

Right *The highly influential 1903 poster by Alfred Roller for the sixteenth Vienna Secession exhibition.*
Collection Merrill C. Berman

The Glasgow School and the Vienna Secession

One cannot discuss the Vienna Secession without briefly acknowledging the influence of the earlier Glasgow School group consisting of Charles Rennie Mackintosh, J. Herbert McNair, and sisters Margaret and Frances Macdonald. The Glasgow School is slightly outside this title's time frame but their graphic work—a sort of geometric take on Art Nouveau with strong architectural overtones (Mackintosh and McNair were architecture students)—set the scene for much of what was to happen later in Germany and Austria, and particularly in Vienna. Curiously, in the U.K. the graphic design of "The Four" was not as popular as their architecture and interior design, but Talwin Morris, art director of Glasgow publisher Blackie's, was an admirer and successfully applied many of their ideas to the mass-market novels, encyclopedias, and dictionaries that formed Blackie's main product lines.

In Austria, on April 3, 1897, the Vienna Secession came into being after a mass resignation by young artists from the Viennese Creative Artists' Association, their principal complaint being the Association's reluctance to accept any new ideas originating from other parts of Europe. The painter Gustav Klimt was a key protagonist, as was the designer Koloman Moser who created some of the movement's best-known pieces, and there are obvious comparisons to be made between their style and that of the Glasgow School. Their exhibition posters provide a guide to the development of the style, gradually moving from the late nineteenth-century symbolist style of illustration to a look which is part Glasgow, part their own take on Art Nouveau. The movement also published its own experimental magazine, *Ver Sacrum* (Sacred Spring) from 1898 until 1903. Design and editorial was handled by a constantly changing group of Secession artists and content was contributed for free.

The style which ultimately defines the Vienna Secession appeared during 1902 with Moser's poster for the thirteenth group exhibition and Alfred Roller's for the fourteenth and sixteenth—the latter being a classic of the style which in the 1960s provided inspiration for psychedelic designers such as Wes Wilson (see page 152). Moser, along with fellow designer Josef Hoffmann, went on to form the *Wiener Werkstätte* (Vienna Workshops) which, somewhat in the spirit of Arts and Crafts movement, produced high-quality furnishings and printed matter until financial difficulties closed them for good in 1932.

Above *Koloman Moser's 1899 cover design for the Secessionists' magazine* Ver Sacrum, *published from 1898 to 1903.*

Art Nouveau

Art Nouveau enjoyed its golden age from 1890 to the early 1910s and is essentially a decorative style rather than a movement with a prescribed philosophy. It is considered a "total" style; its application was used to great effect in architecture and furniture design as well as graphic design for posters and advertisements. The popularity in Europe of all things Japanese during the late nineteenth century provided early points of reference and the style drew much of its inspiration from Japanese *Ukiyo-e* woodblock printing. Art Nouveau is easily identified by its elegant flowing look; it displays a natural, organic quality with flowers, trees, and vines featuring regularly in borders and illustrations alongside the female form, another frequently used Art Nouveau motif.

The importance of Art Nouveau lies not only in its decorative qualities as it was also instrumental in helping to bridge the gap between the historical revival styles that had dominated printed graphics in the nineteenth century and the radical new styles of the Modern movement which were to follow. Commercial artists working in this attractive style were able to inject a significant amount of visual appeal into printed mass communication by fusing the painterly qualities of "art" with illustration, aided by the latest advances in commercial color printing techniques.

Above *The 1897 poster by Alphonse Mucha displays many of the typical features of the Art Nouveau style—the organic forms and the central female figure—but unusually for him, also includes inset images in a traditional engraved style. This may have been a stipulation of the client.*

Right *The "total" style of Art Nouveau is demonstrated clearly by Emmanuel Orazi's 1905 poster for Parisian gallery La Maison Moderne (The Modern House). All the objects illustrated in the poster, including the jewelry worn by the woman, are Art Nouveau-style creations.*

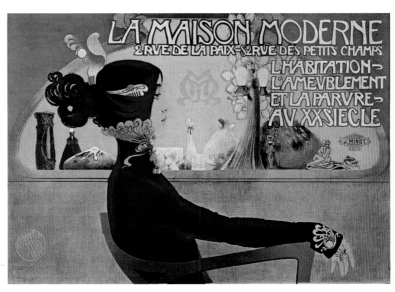

Plakatstil (Sachplakat)

Plakatstil (German for "poster style") is a distinctive flat-color illustration approach which originated in Germany in the mid-1900s. Also occasionally referred to as *Sachplakat* (or "object-poster") in Switzerland, Plakatstil reflects a pared-back graphic style pioneered by The Beggarstaffs—the collective pseudonym of William Nicholson and James Pryde—in the 1890s. It was pioneered by the young commercial artist Lucian Bernhard (see pages 38–9) after he entered a competition to design a poster advertising Priester matches. The omission of decorative borders and florid details marks the style as the first to challenge the dominance of Art Nouveau in Europe, and in some ways represents a visual transition from Art Nouveau to the Modernist styles that were to follow. The *Priester*

Above *The Beggarstaffs—a partnership between artists William Nicholson and James Pryde—preempted* Plakatstil *by a number of years. They worked primarily in collage and cut paper and achieved little commercial success at the time, but their work, including their 1895 poster* Lyceum Don Quixote, *is now considered to be highly influential.*

Left *Emil Cardinaux's Zermatt poster of 1908 is considered to be the first example of Sachplakat, the Swiss version of Germany's* Plakatstil.

poster and others like it, which feature only the product image and name, imply a no-frills confidence in a company's product that has become a key component of modern advertising technique. Plakatstil style does not compete for attention with the subject of the poster; its simplicity helps to emphasize it.

Ernst Growald, the man who had first proclaimed Bernhard a design genius, shrewdly contracted a number of other designers who had started to work in the Plakatstil manner to his print firm Hollerbaum & Schmidt. These included Hans Rudi Erdt, Julius Gipkens, and Julius Klinger. Due to the immense popularity of the style, the designers enjoyed a constant workload, and Hollerbaum & Schmidt became one of the most prestigious publishers of posters in Germany at that time.

Will H. Bradley earns his place in the history of graphic design as the main exponent of both the Arts and Crafts movement and the emerging Art Nouveau style in turn-of-the-century America. Born in Boston in 1868, Bradley moved to Michigan with his mother at age nine after his father's death, and was apprenticed to a printer at the early age of twelve. Like many early graphic design pioneers, he received no formal design training. Instead, Bradley drew his ideas from books and magazines featuring articles about emerging design styles in Europe and from his admiration of Japanese woodblock printing, which provided much of the early inspiration for Art Nouveau. He was also affected profoundly by the work of William Morris and his efforts with the Kelmscott Press, and resolved to one day set up a private press of his own.

Above *Hans Rudi Erdt's reassuring poster of 1911, executed in the Plakatstil style for the Never Fail safe company.*

After taking unpaid internships with Chicago engraving firm J. Manz & Co and with Rand McNally, Bradley moved to Chicago permanently in 1886 and by 1889 he had become a freelance graphic designer with a growing roster of clients that would soon include the important trade journal *Inland Printer*, literary magazine *The Chap Book*, and *Vogue*. He exhibited his work prolifically during this time, taking part in Chicago's fourth and fifth Annual Black and White Exhibitions and the 1893 World's Columbian Exposition where he gained valuable exposure.

Above *Bradley illustrated many covers for* Collier's National Weekly *magazine during his career. The example is the Christmas 1907 edition.*

Left *A promotional poster for* Bradley: His Book, Will Bradley, 1896.

Bradley's illustrative style utilized boldly contrasting asymmetrical and curvilinear shapes, held together with areas of black and white and strong, flat color. Indeed, Bradley is widely credited with popularizing the flat-color style in the United States and earned the nickname the "Dean of American Designers".

The rapid improvements in color lithography around the turn of the century meant that many more poster commissions were available on both sides of the Atlantic. It became fashionable in the U.S. to collect Art Nouveau posters by European artists, such as Henri de Toulouse-Lautrec, and Bradley was able to capitalize by producing his own unique pieces in the Art Nouveau style which garnered favorable reviews. However, his principal source of work came from magazines where he would design both the covers and interiors, and this success enabled him to fulfill his ambition and establish the Wayside Press after moving to Springfield, Massachusetts in 1895. From 1896 to 1898 Bradley published his own art and literary magazine titled *Bradley: His Book*, but overwork caused a him to suffer from a physical collapse in 1897, leading to the sale of the Wayside Press. He went on to serve as advertising art director for American Type Founders from 1903 to 1905, where he both wrote and produced twelve editions of their promotional publication *The American Chap Book*. Following this period he acted as art editor for a number of significant magazines including *Colliers*, where his own cover illustrations and those he commissioned led to increased sales of the national weekly. Bradley ended his professional career at Hearst Publications art directing magazines such as *Century*, *Good Housekeeping*, *Metropolitan*, *Pearson's*, and *Success* before retiring in 1928, but continued to design and write until his death in 1962 at the age of 93.

Peter Behrens

The Arts and Crafts movement under William Morris and the all-encompassing "total design" ideals of Art Nouveau held a significant relevancy for designers across Europe, and German architect and designer Peter Behrens was no exception. A proponent of the Art Nouveau style, or *Jugendstil* as it was called in Germany, the self-taught Behrens originally studied painting in his native Hamburg before relocating to Munich. In 1899 he was invited to design and build a villa at the famous artist's colony in Darmstadt and, over a period of several years, produced a building which conformed to the ideals of equal importance and complete coordination in every aspect of the design. Absolutely everything in the house was designed by Behrens, including the towels! Ultimately, the project guided him towards a more austere approach to design but the idea of completeness stayed with him and informed much of his later work.

Behrens believed that, after architecture, typography provided the key visual component for any given design period, and experimented widely with new typefaces and alternative approaches to layout. In 1900 he designed the booklet pictured above titled *Feste des Lebens und der Kunst: Eine Betrachtung des Theaters als Höchsten Kultursymbols* (Celebration of Life and Art: A Consideration of the Theater as the Highest Symbol of a Culture). It is thought to be the first instance of sans-serif type used as running text in a book layout—a significant moment in graphic design by any standards.

By 1903 he had been appointed director of Düsseldorf's *Kunstgewerbeschule* (School of Arts and Crafts), and in 1907 was one of the key founding members of the *Deutscher Werkbund* (German Association of Craftsmen), a modernizing organization which would later play its own part in the

formation of the Bauhaus school of design in Germany. It is notable that from 1907 Behrens employed a number of assistants including Ludwig Mies van der Rohe, Le Corbusier (the adopted name used by Charles-Édouard Jeanneret-Gris), Adolf Meyer, and Walter Gropius, all of whom were influenced by Behrens's ideas and would play major roles in the development of design and architecture during the following decades.

In the same year, 1907, Behrens was retained by the large electrical goods manufacturer AEG (Allgemeine Elektrizitäts-Gesellschaft) as their artistic consultant. His role developed rapidly from overseeing the design of their literature and advertising to a complete coordinated redesign of AEG's logotype, publicity material, and subsequently its branded products. Through this work, Behrens is credited as the first designer to create what we would today refer to as a corporate identity. By creating visual consistency across all manufactured goods, AEG's products became instantly recognizable to the general public and the company benefited greatly from the consumer confidence which grew from the qualities implied by Behrens's attention to detail. His design brief even extended to AEG buildings; given that Behrens was also an architect, he was well placed to

design the new AEG Turbine Factory in Berlin during 1908–9. The building remains intact today and is an important early example of industrial classicism.

He also designed a number of typefaces for the Klingspor Type Foundry including Behrens-Schrift, Behrens-Antiqua, and Behrens-Mediaeval. The AEG identity utilized Behrens-Antiqua as its principal typeface across all printed literature.

Behrens produced hardly any graphic design after 1914 and the outbreak of World War One, choosing instead to concentrate on architectural work, but the relatively brief period he spent as a commercial artist was hugely influential. He died in Berlin in 1940 at the age of 71.

Opposite *The title pages from Behrens's 1900 work* Feste des Lebens und der Kunst: Eine Betrachtung des Theaters als höchsten Kultursymbols, *thought to be the first use of sans-serif type as running text in a book.*

Right *A poster for AEG, designed in 1910, to advertise their range of electric lamps.*

Lucian Bernhard

Lucian Bernhard's initial contribution to graphic design was as one of the first commercial artists to reject the ornamental dominance of Art Nouveau during the 1900s. His path to graphic design fame makes for an unusual story as he was born in Stuttgart in 1883 as Emil Kahn. It is not entirely clear why he chose to change his name but his family were not supportive of his original career decision to become an artist, so he may have simply wanted to make a clean start.

The first big break for the untrained but talented Bernhard came about when he entered a contest to design a poster for Priester matches in 1905, having moved to Berlin two years earlier. Today this type of competition would be treated with outright suspicion but in 1905 there was no established network of graphics professionals to consult, so design contests were fairly popular as a way of acquiring commissions. His first draft for the design was a busy composition featuring a checkered tablecloth and a lit cigar propped in an ashtray with smoke rising to transform into a backdrop of dancing girls. After deciding the girls were too much, he painted them out; then a friend made the observation that his work looked like an advertisement for cigars so the cigar was painted out too; and finally the ashtray and tablecloth were also

eliminated, leaving just a pair of matches with the single word "Priester" added above in Bernhard's distinctive calligraphic style.

His hastily prepared and, it has to be said, haphazardly conceived poster was first rejected by the panel of judges and was literally thrown into a trashcan. It was subsequently rescued by jury member Ernst Growald of the lithography firm Hollerbaum & Schmidt, who stated "This is my first prize! Here is a genius." And thus, one of the most famous posters of all time was created and Plakatstil was born. Bernhard had unwittingly raised the bar on a style which would influence designers for generations to come, consequently moving graphics away from the more naturalistic Art Nouveau. He went on to achieve significant commercial success, opening his own studio in 1906 and becoming one of the founder members of the Deutscher Werkbund along with Peter Behrens (see pages 36–7) in 1907. He produced hundreds of posters, packing design concepts, and trademarks during his career, and his lettering style attracted the attention of type foundries such as Berthold in Berlin, and Flinsch in Frankfurt who commissioned and issued the well-known Bernhard Antiqua in 1912. Over a dozen further typefaces or typeface families were to follow, with Bernhard continuing to attract commissions from foundries well into the 1930s. He also studied carpentry in order to add furniture design to his roster of services, and architecture, which led to designs for both houses and industrial buildings. Bernhard died in New York in 1972.

Left *Bernhard's style was so distinctive that he rarely strayed from it, as witnessed by this 1909 poster for Adler typewriters.*

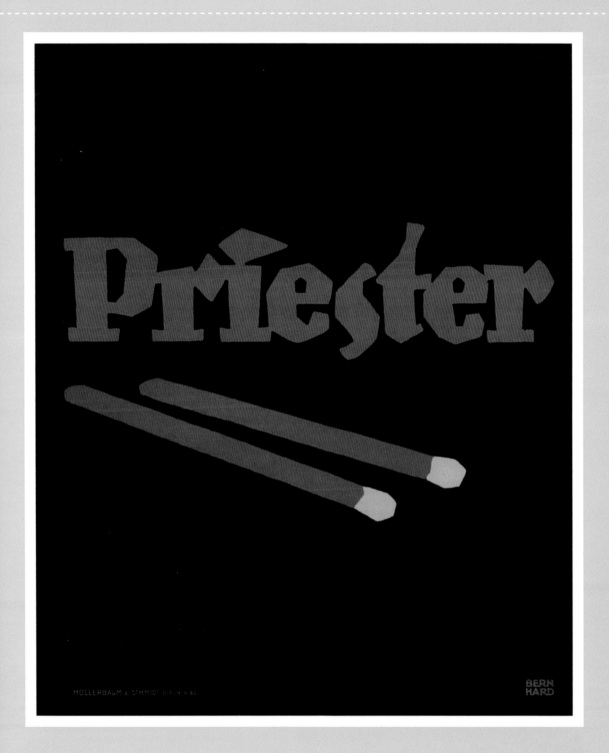

Above *Bernhard's famous poster designed in 1905 for Priester matches. The simplicity of the execution is credited with launching the Plakatstil style in Germany.*

Clearface

Arnold Boecklin

Windsor

Village

Della Robbia

*News Gothic

Eckmann

Century Old Style

Franklin Gothic

COPPERPLATE GOTHIC

Graphic style occupied two distinct camps at the turn of the century and type design fell into line with the traditional versus progressive aesthetic of the early 1900s. Typefaces with a hand-drawn historical flavor supported the Arts and Crafts and Art Nouveau movements, whilst sans-serifs (or gothics) were championed by the modernist movements emerging in both Europe and North America. Here is a list of the most notable typefaces.

Eckmann
Otto Eckmann | 1900

Copperplate Gothic
Frederic W. Goudy | 1901

Della Robbia
Thomas Maitland Cleland | 1902

Franklin Gothic
Morris Fuller Benton | 1902–5

Village
Frederic W. Goudy | 1903

Windsor
Eleisha Pechey | 1903

Arnold Boecklin
Otto Weisert | 1904

Century Old Style
Morris Fuller Benton | 1905

Clearface
Morris Fuller Benton | 1905–07

News Gothic
Morris Fuller Benton | 1908

Key typefaces

Franklin Gothic

ABCDEFGHIJKLM
NOPQRSTUVWXYZ
abcdefghijklm
nopqrstuvwxyz
1234567890
(.,:;?!$£&-*){ÀOÜÇ}

In the 1900s, American Type Founders (ATF) was the largest commercial type foundry in the world. Its chief designer, Morris Fuller Benton, designed Franklin Gothic in 1902 and the typeface was released in 1905. In the days of hot metal it took some considerable time to cut and cast a typeface prior to its first commercial release. Franklin Gothic, named after Benjamin Franklin, is considered to be one of the most venerable of the American gothic typefaces. It is generally believed to have been inspired, at least in part, by the Berthold Type Foundry's Akzidenz-Grotesk from 1896. As an American equivalent it can certainly be seen as equally successful, and is widely used to this day. Its thick strokes, wide capitals, and good legibility make it popular with magazine and newspaper designers.

Clearface

ABCDEFGHIJKLM
NOPQRSTUVWXYZ
abcdefghijklm
nopqrstuvwxyz
1234567890
(.,:;?!$£&-*){ÀOÜÇ}

Clearface is another of Morris Fuller Benton's typefaces, released by American Type Founders in 1907 and designed as a collaboration with his father Linn Boyd Benton. Benton senior had been the co-owner of the Benton, Waldo & Co. Type Foundry which was part of the original merger of companies that formed the ATC in 1892. Work began on the design of the face in 1905, with the regular weight being the first commercial release two years later. The family was later expanded to include bold and heavy weights. It was a highly regarded typeface in its time and was licensed to all the major manufacturers of composing machines, including Linotype and Monotype. A distinctive and functional typeface with high legibility, it remains popular with designers who wish to evoke an early twentieth century aesthetic.

Steinlen's lettering style, while still decorative, is less ornate than that of many of his contemporaries such as **Alphonse Mucha** and Henri Privat-Livemont.

The decorative elements are present, such as in this "halo" behind the cat's head, but are less organic in nature than typical Art Nouveau ornamentation.

The illustrative style of Steinlen's posters, particularly those produced for the Parisian entertainment establishment Le Chat Noir, are strongly reminiscent of the **Japanese Ukiyo-e** woodblock prints which influenced the Art Nouveau style.

Steinlen's posters often feature **large areas of flat color**. The tendency of many artists working in the Art Nouveau style was to fill every available space with ornate decoration.

Cabaret du Chat Noir

Théophile Steinlen | 1896

Théophile Steinlen posters provide a distinct contrast to those of his fellow designers from this period, such as Alphonse Mucha. Steinlen's posters are less packed with ornate detail—they often feature large areas of flat color free from decoration—and are essentially more faithful to the Japanese *Ukiyo-e* woodblock print style from which Art Nouveau draws much of its original influence. His posters for Le Chat Noir (The Black Cat), one of the original cabarets situated in Paris's Montmartre district, represent his best-known work and are still reproduced in large numbers to this day. In fact, there is one hanging on the wall beside my desk as I type this.

Steinlen was born in Lausanne, Switzerland, in 1859 and moved to Paris in his early twenties, where he settled within the artistic community in and around Montmartre, painted prolifically, and continued to nurture his great fondness for cats. He was also a harsh critic of the grimness of life for many people living in Paris and produced numerous works illustrating the shortcomings of Parisian society. Steinlen died in 1923.

The color palette row below is a sampler of colors selected from the *Cabaret du Chat Noir* poster shown here, and is representative of the range of colors a designer working in this style might have used during the 1900s.

c =	000%	000%	005%	020%	000%	000%	060%	000%
m =	005%	015%	025%	055%	075%	085%	045%	000%
y =	070%	070%	075%	070%	080%	090%	075%	000%
k =	000%	000%	000%	000%	000%	000%	045%	100%

1910s

Graphic design during the 1910s is notably affected by the Great War, or World War One as it became known after 1939. Following the assassination of Archduke Franz Ferdinand in Sarajevo on June 28, 1914, the war was fought along a line passing through Belgium and northeastern France and ended with the truce of November 11, 1918. Given that a large portion of Europe's collective financial resources was directed at the war effort, the world economy was thrown into chaos during this period.

The decade is nonetheless regarded as a period of massive industrial advancement, particularly in America, which did not enter the War until April 1917, and not solely because of the rapid technological advances that normally accompany large-scale warfare. In many ways the U.S. had come of age on the world stage during the early 1910s, becoming the most highly industrialized country in the world and controlling around 35 percent of the world's export market for manufactured goods by 1913. This figure more than doubles that achieved by either Germany or the U.K., the other highest-performing exporters prior to the outbreak of the war. The period also marks the earliest point at which American popular culture, alongside manufactured goods, started to become a lucrative national product. American music, dance, and fashion styles began to make serious inroads into the consciousness of people all over Europe. All the same, industry was hit hard by the war and the commercial development of graphic design slowed as a consequence.

The massive social and cultural upheaval experienced in Europe was not altogether lost on artists and designers. While the Futurist poets (see right) continued to steer attitudes to graphic design style in a radical direction, the Dadaists (see page 47) were turning typographic standards on their head, and on the back of the crushing revolution that ended this tumultuous decade the Russian Constructivists (see pages 62–5) created their own distinctive style of graphic design referencing the Cubist-influenced paintings of artists such as Pablo Picasso and Georges Braque.

Futurism and Vorticism

Futurism began not as a visually artistic movement, but in the form of Italian poet Filippo Marinetti's *Manifesto of Futurism*, published in the Paris newspaper *Le Figaro* on February 20, 1909. Shocking even by today's standards, the content of the manifesto proclaimed an enthusiasm for the modern life in a very aggressive manner—extolling the virtues of machines, speed, and violent revolt. Futurist poets began to write without adherence to the rules of grammar and their own visual interpretations of their poetry took on a chaotic form which followed no structural constraints.

Futurism enjoys a more popular association with painters but was nonetheless enormously influential for graphic designers at the time. Collage techniques were used to paste together typographic compositions, reproduced using photoengraved plates rather than traditionally set type. In typographic terms, this work was arguably the most radically experimental since movable type had been invented over 400 years earlier. Futurist subjects were typically gritty urban scenes that emphasized the themes of modern technology such as machines, speed, war, and physical force; often painted in a style molded strongly by Cubism. Associated graphic design pieces follow a similar signature theme with bold typography arranged in a seemingly random fashion, strong focal points, and high-contrast color palettes.

Marinetti's famous *Zang Tumb Tumb* poem recounting the Battle of Adrianople was published in book form in 1914 and is recognized as the first example of Futurist-influenced graphic design. Marinetti held an idealized view of war as a positive force for change which would somehow prepare Italy for a modern, industrialized future by eradicating its fixation with the past—a view not necessarily shared by the majority of Futurist designers. In line with other influential artistic styles, commercial adoption of Futurism was not immediate, occurring mainly during the 1920s. Designer Fortunato Depero's theater posters, book and magazine covers, and advertisements are prominent examples.

Left *The cover of Filippo Marinetti's 1914 publication* Zang Tumb Tumb, *a futurist poem based on his personal experience fighting in the Battle of Adrianople during the Balkan War of 1912–13.*

Soaring to Success !

DAILY HERALD

— the Early Bird.

In England, artists of a similar anarchistic ilk chose the alternative term Vorticism for their brand of Cubist-influenced painting and graphic design. In the summer of 1914, the painter Wyndham Lewis published the first of two important journals promoting the style. The second, and final, edition was published a year later. Titled *Blast*, the name was derived from Lewis's quote of wanting to "blast years 1837–1900," or, in other words, to drive out the conservatism of the Victorian era. The principal difference between Futurism and Vorticism is that the latter eschews the frenetic movement implied by Futurist style in favor of a more static form of composition, where the movement is implied by the power of juxtaposed or angled objects and type. Vorticism was short-lived, ostensibly because of the difficulties created by the war, but its influence on graphic design was extensive. The work of Edward McKnight Kauffer (see pages 92–3) provides key examples, particularly in his *Soaring to Success! Daily Herald—the Early Bird* poster which was published in 1919 using an image which McKnight Kauffer had first drawn three years earlier.

Above *Edward McKnight Kauffer's* Soaring to Success! Daily Herald–the Early Bird *poster of 1919 features a Vorticist illustration created several years earlier.*

Right *The cover design of Wyndham Lewis's second edition of* Blast, *published in 1915.*

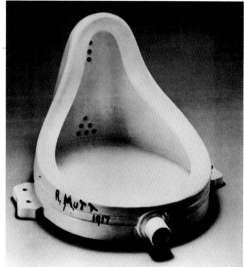

Above *The Dada "sculpture"* Fountain *by Marcel Duchamp, 1917.*

Right *Hannah Höch's 1919 collage typifies her work in the Dada style and carries the wonderful title* Cut with a Kitchen Knife Dada through the Last Weimar Beer-Belly Cultural Epoch of Germany.

Dada

Dada was, in a nutshell, anti-war. It was more or less anti-everything, excepting its wish to draw attention to what it summed up as the impoverishment of cultural life as a result of the violence of World War One. Like Futurism, Dada began as a literary movement, following the launch of the Cabaret Voltaire club in Zurich, Switzerland in February 1916 by the poet Hugo Ball. The artist Marcel Duchamp was one of the movement's most prominent spokesman and is well known for his 1917 attributed sculpture *Fountain* which was simply a urinal, rotated through 90° and signed "R. Mutt 1917." The piece, the original of which is now lost, was typical of Dada's philosophy which sought not to create art in a traditional sense but to use artistic expression to deride a society which they felt had lost its way.

Dada's influence on graphic design is not necessarily the easiest to spot as the association is as much about attitude as it is about visual style. Its direct impact on design manifests in the way the vocabulary of Dada, particularly in terms of

typography, provided designers with a new set of visual tools to work with. Indirectly, it encouraged designers to change the way they observed existing styles and inspired them to think of new ways to adapt them for their own work.

Like Futurism, Dada did not begin to leave its mark on commercial graphic design immediately. Dadaists such as Raoul Hausmann, Hannah Höch, and Kurt Schwitters were key pioneers of the Photomontage style which enjoyed its heyday throughout the 1920s. Schwitters even created his own movement within Dada, named Merz (from the German word *Kommerz* meaning "commerce;"), using mainly collage to create graphic images from printed ephemera and other found materials. He continued to apply elements of Dada typographic style to his work while running his own design studio from 1923 to 1932, combining Dada with the emerging Constructivist style.

Propaganda (part one)

World War One was fought on an unprecedented scale, largely by civilian volunteers or conscripts rather than professional soldiers. Britain maintained the smallest professional army of any European power at the outbreak of the war, while other countries such as Germany and France already had national service in place, so in August 1914 the Parliamentary Recruiting Committee was established and handed the responsibility for the production of all war posters in Britain. Enthusiasm to sign up and do one's bit ran high during the early days of the war, but as stories of the horror of the trenches filtered back, the difficulties in persuading men to enlist grew, and compulsory conscription was finally introduced in 1916.

All countries involved in the conflict produced propaganda posters with differing design styles reflective of national identity, but the message was common—they tended to focus on the human-centered aspects of war using a combination of persuasive psychology and potential guilt. A well-known example of this approach can be seen in Savile Lumley's 1914 poster *Daddy, what did YOU do in the Great War?* which plays directly on the notion that men would be unable to face their children in the future if they did not join up. Drawn in a "boy's own" comic form, the style in which Lumley generally worked, the image was extremely potent and reportedly very effective. An American example sometimes credited with beginning to turn opinion in the U.S. in favor of direct involvement in the war is Frederick Spear's 1915 poster *Enlist*. It depicts a drowning woman holding a child in her arms and was published after the RMS *Lusitania* was sunk off the Irish coast by a German U-boat in May 1915. Of the 1,105 passengers and crew that lost their lives, 128 were American—including Elbert Hubbard (see page 30), the founder of the Roycroft Press. The image, inspired by a contemporary newspaper report of the sinking, was extremely shocking for its time.

The most famous British poster of all is probably Alfred Leete's *Britons, [Lord Kitchener] wants YOU*, designed in 1914. Kitchener was secretary of state for war, highly respected, and so well known that his portrait replaced the actual words "Lord Kitchener" in the center of the poster. The design was adapted from a cover for the monthly magazine *London Opinion* and stylistically is fairly plain, supporting the general abandonment at that time of decorative styles such as Art Nouveau in favor of a more direct realism.

Daddy, what did YOU do in the Great War?

The Parliamentary Recruiting Committee's tastes were conservative. They preferred posters designed using traditional styling and tended to commission directly from printing firms who also provided design services without involving the creative talents of a commercial artist. In fact, the practical needs of wartime poster production prevented the furtherance of graphic design as a commercial industry during, and immediately after, the war. In America, James Montgomery Flagg designed the counterpart for Leete's poster in 1917, creating the equally famous poster where Uncle Sam states "I Want YOU for U.S. Army."

In Germany, propaganda posters generally retained the styles of the time and were often designed in the Plakatstil style by well-known designers such as Lucian Bernhard (see pages 38–9), Ludwig Hohlwein (see page 52), and Hans Rudi Erdt, whose 1917 poster *U-Boote Heraus!* is a common example. Somewhat ironically, the posters were criticized after the war for being overly stylish and failing to communicate the importance of the message. Adolf Hitler is known to have admired the ruthlessness of British propaganda's central message, something which would become all too apparent twenty years later.

The topic of graphic design as propaganda in the context of World War Two is continued on page 110.

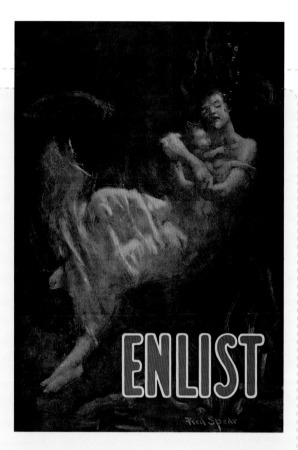

Opposite *Saville Lumley's cleverly conceived study of guilt at not serving one's country, the 1914 British recruitment poster* Daddy, what did YOU do in the Great War?

Above right *American illustrator Frederick Spear's poster* Enlist *was inspired directly by the sinking of the RMS Lusitania in May 1915, an event that caused the deaths of 128 American citizens.*

Right U-Boats Out!, *a German poster issued in 1916 and designed by Hans Rudi Erdt. German propaganda posters from World War One were often designed in the Plakatstil manner.*

The London Underground

This profile is essentially about a transportation company but collectively it is about a number of extremely important individuals brought together by one insightful visionary named Frank Pick. The London Underground (originally the Metropolitan Railway) began transporting passengers around subterranean London as early as 1863 and during its early years the company's promotional efforts were, at best, disjointed. Pick, a qualified solicitor and administrator, was already working for London Underground when he was handed the publicity role in 1908. His strong personal interest in art and design and a desire to eradicate the visual mishmash of advertising posters and signage that littered the walls of the stations, led to one of the most successful and enduring corporate design programs in history.

Pick first rationalized the company's advertising policy by introducing poster boards that were manufactured to designated sizes and affixed at specific locations within London Underground properties and stations. Prior to this, posters had simply been pasted on whatever space was available, leading to complaints from passengers that it was often difficult to locate the signage indicating the names of the stations. Navigation systems were also gradually improved and the first station signs, a red disk with a single blue bar and white sans-serif lettering, evolved by 1916 into the famous logo designed by the calligrapher Edward Johnston. This logo is still in use today, having been refined slightly in 1972. Johnston also designed Underground, a typeface for exclusive use by London Underground that appeared on all signage and publicity material. Originally the face was not licensed to any type foundries, to ensure that the London Underground posters would not be mistaken for other company's advertisements, but it is now available as P22 Underground (see page 57), a commercial font licensed via the P22 Foundry and The London Transport Museum in 1997, and as a variant named ITC Johnston which was first released in 1999 and updated again in 2009.

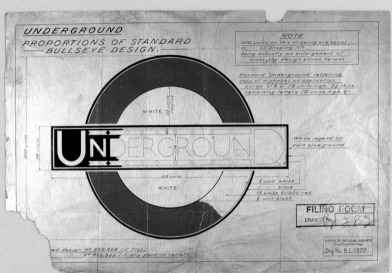

The subway posters themselves, all of which were personally commissioned by Pick during his tenure, were designed and illustrated to reflect the popular graphic styles of the day and remain highly collectable. Designers chosen by Pick during the early years included Edward McKnight Kauffer (see pages

92–3), Alfred Leete, Austin Cooper, Horace Taylor, Charles Paine, and Frederick Charles Herrick. The subjects were rarely focused on the company itself but rather on the destinations and what each had to offer, such as theaters, museums, sporting venues, exhibitions, and parks. In this sense, the posters were acting more as public information notices than advertising, but the results were often striking and the public reception was resoundingly positive. One particular poster that did break the mold was the *Wonderground Map of London* illustrated by Max Gill, Eric Gill's younger brother. Designed with the intention of providing some humorous relief for commuters in 1914, the highly detailed map was displayed in every station and was a huge hit, becoming the first Underground poster to be sold commercially as a reproduction.

Pick rose through the ranks, becoming London Underground's managing director in 1928. He continued to influence every aspect of the Underground's design philosophy, leaving behind a hugely important example of how to implement a corporate design program effectively and responsibly.

Opposite above *Edward Johnston's original drawings for the design of the London Underground roundel, 1918.*

Opposite below *A detail from the 1914 poster* Wonderground Map of London *illustrated by Max Gill, younger brother of the better-known designer Eric Gill.*

Above Underground to Wood Lane *by Frederick Charles Herrick, 1920. The poster is a fine example of the way the company advertised events that could be reached by Underground rather than directly promoting the company itself.*

Ludwig Hohlwein

Above *Hohlwein's 1915 poster for the People's Charity for Prisoners of War. The abstraction of Plakatstil was later deemed too stylish a choice for posters which were intended to tug at the heartstrings of the general public.*

Born in Munich in 1874, Ludwig Hohlwein was a noted poster designer, working primarily in the Plakatstil or Sachplakat style pioneered by Lucian Bernhard (see page 38–9). Like many of his contemporaries Hohlwein was architecturally trained, but began his design career around 1904 as an illustrator on the German magazine *Jugend* (the source of the German term for Art Nouveau, Jugendstil). His work differed from other notable Plakatstil designers in that he incorporated more texture and tonal contrast in his painted images. The distinctive flat shapes that distinguish the style are still very much in evidence in his work but the level of detail is generally greater and rather more painterly. His earlier posters, often commissioned by retailers, display less of this characteristic but during the war years he produced several notable posters in support of fundraising for wounded German veterans which began to demonstrate an increasingly more naturalistic style—almost akin to a combination of Plakatstil and Art Nouveau.

Hohlwein enjoyed considerable success during the interwar years, providing poster designs for the flourishing advertising industry and further refining his distinctive hybrid style. Towards the end of his career he attracted the attention of the Nazi party for whom he designed a number of powerfully graphic and overtly nationalistic posters. The designs are as fine as ever but, due to their subject matter, the work sadly sullies what is otherwise a distinguished body of work. He died in Berchtesgaden, Germany in 1949.

El Lissitzky

In common with many of the early design innovators, the great Russian designer El (Lazar Markovich) Lissitzky came from a multidisciplinary background which included firstly architecture, then graphic design and photography, plus furniture and exhibition design. He was born near Smolensk in 1890 and in 1909 relocated to Darmstadt in Germany to study architectural engineering—a field which would continue to influence his work throughout his life. It was quite normal at the time for Russian Jews to travel abroad to study, as the Russian Empire limited the number of university places available to Jewish students.

In 1919, Lissitzky was invited by the painter Marc Chagall to take up a teaching post at Vitebsk art school near Moscow. While there, he developed his own painting stye which he named PROUN (an acronym for the Russian phrase "project for the affirmation of the new"), which added a form of three-dimensional, illusionary effect to the totally flat style which enjoyed widespread popularity at that time. This architecturally informed painting style would go on to directly affect his graphic design work, an early and famous example being his 1919 poster *Beat the Whites with the Red Wedge*. He supported the aims of the Bolsheviks' 1917 revolution (the Bolsheviks were a faction of the Marxist Russian Social Democratic Party), seeing it as a new start for Russia, and the poster illustrates his support for the "Reds" against the anti-communist "Whites."

Throughout the 1920s, Lissitzky participated in *De Stijl* (Dutch for "The Style") artistic movement (see page 67), collaborated with the Dadaists (see page 47), and paid frequent visits to Germany's famous Bauhaus school (see page 68–70), where he lectured. His extensive interest in typography grew to become the dominant element in much of his work during this time and the prolificacy of his output made him one of Europe's foremost advocates of Supremacist and Constructivist styles. He contracted pulmonary tuberculosis in 1923 after a bout of pneumonia and died in Moscow in 1941 at the tragically early age of only 51.

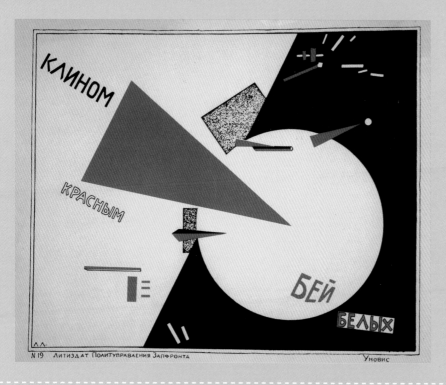

Left *Arguably one of El Lissitzky's best-known pieces,* Beat the Whites with the Red Wedge *was designed in 1919 and depicts the struggle between the Bolshevik army and Alexander Kerensky's Socialists.*

Souvenir

Centaur

Bernhard

Goudy O

Cloister Old

MAXIMIL
ANTIQUA

Cooper Old

Undergro

Antiqua

d Style

Style

AN

*

Style

und

Kennerley Old Style

Plantin

The 1910s represent a somewhat turbulent period for type design with the Futurists turning to hand-drawn typography and highly experimental typefaces and layout techniques, mixing faces and point sizes in previously untried combinations. However, the rapid development of print technology and typesetting techniques continued apace and a number of beautiful, classic serif faces from the likes of Frederic Goudy and Bruce Rogers emerged during this decade.

Kennerley Old Style
Frederic W. Goudy | 1911

Bernhard Antiqua
Lucian Bernhard | 1912

Centaur
Bruce Rogers | 1914

Cloister Old Style
Morris Fuller Benton | 1913

Maximilian Antiqua
Rudolf Koch | 1914

Plantin
Frank Hinman Pierpont | 1913

Souvenir
Morris Fuller Benton | 1914

Goudy Old Style
Frederic W. Goudy | 1915

Underground
Edward Johnston | 1916
(Now available as P22 Underground and ITC Johnston as shown on this spread)

Cooper Old Style
Oswald B. Cooper | 1919

Bernhard Antiqua

ABCDEFGHIJKLM

NOPQRSTUVWXYZ

abcdefghijklm

nopqrstuvwxyz

1234567890

(.,:;?!$£&-*){ÀÓÜÇ}

Designers working in the Plakatstil or Sachplakat style (see page 33) were instrumental in popularizing Roman lettering in Germany—blackletter type was previously the norm. Lucian Bernhard (see pages 38–9) was a key protagonist of Plakatstil and his distinctive lettering style was used as the basis for several popular typefaces of the time. Bernhard Antiqua was published by Frankfurt's Flinsch foundry in 1912 and was based on the lettering from his famous *Priester* matches poster designed in 1905. The original typeface was impressively faithful to Bernhard's hand-drawn letterforms and represents the visual feel of the period extremely well. Unfortunately, the digital version available today is limited to Bernhard Condensed Bold, as shown here, but the spirit of the original remains in the revised font.

Centaur

ABCDEFGHIJKLM

NOPQRSTUVWXYZ

abcdefghijklm

nopqrstuvwxyz

1234567890

(.,:;?!$£&-*){ÀÓÜÇ}

Bruce Rogers, the designer of the beautiful Centaur typeface, was a renowned American book designer active from 1895 until his death in 1957. The typeface was created as a commission from the Metropolitan Museum of Art for its Museum Press and was based on Nicolas Jenson's typeface of 1470. Jenson's work has been referenced by several designers over the years but Centaur is regarded by many as the finest interpretation. It was first used in 1914 in a limited edition of *The Centaur* by Maurice de Guérin, providing the typeface with its name. When the type was released commercially some fourteen years later the italic was designed for Monotype by Frederic Warde, basing it on his own drawings for the typeface Arrighi. With its open character forms and low contrast, Centaur remains popular with book designers.

Underground

ABCDEFGHIJKLM
NOPQRSTUVWXYZ
abcdefghijklm
nopqrstuvwxyz
1234567890
(.,:;?!$£&-*){ÀÓÜÇ}

In 1913, London Underground's Frank Pick (see pages 50–1) commissioned calligrapher Edward Johnston to design an exclusive typeface for use by the company on its posters and signage. This famous typeface, introduced in 1916, was originally named Underground but eventually became known simply as Johnston and is an integral element of London Underground's visual identity. The sample shown here is ITC Johnston, a digital variant of the original font. It was drawn by British designers Richard Dawson and Dave Farey in 1999 and is somewhat closer in style to the original than New Johnston, designed in 1979 by Elichi Kono at Banks & Miles for London Underground and currently still in use by the company. In particular, the numerals "1" and "4" featured in ITC Johnston are faithful to Johnston's 1916 typeface.

Cooper Old Style

ABCDEFGHIJKLM
NOPQRSTUVWXYZ
abcdefghijklm
nopqrstuvwxyz
1234567890
(.,:;?!$£&-*){ÀÓÜÇ}

Oswald Bruce Cooper studied under the great Frederic Goudy at Chicago's Frank Holme School and in 1904 formed Bertsch & Cooper with business partner Fred Bertsch. The company produced newspaper advertisements, magazine and book layouts, and Cooper specialized in hand-lettering. Following commercial success in this area with lettering licensed as commercial typefaces by the larger foundries, Cooper designed Cooper Old Style in 1919, adding an italic weight five years later. The typeface is probably the first ever to be drawn with rounded serifs so is somewhat of a milestone, and the family grew to include another well-known variant, Cooper Black, which was equally successful.

8. Kriegsanleihe (8th War Loan)

Julius Klinger | 1917

Julius Klinger was an Austrian painter and commercial artist. He received his education in Vienna at the Technologisches Gewerbemuseum before relocating to Berlin in the late 1890s where he became one of the group of Plakatstil poster artists placed under contract to the Hollerbaum and Schmidt printing firm. Other members of the group included Lucian Bernhard, Hans Rudi Erdt, and Julius Gipkens. Klinger arrived at his Plakatstil-influenced style after first becoming involved with the Vienna Secessionist movement in his home town.

Klinger's World War One posters retained the Plakatstil very closely, relying on simplified but dynamic shapes and strong flat colors to broadcast the powerful messages conveyed in his posters. The example shown here for the *8. Kriegsanleihe*, which translates as the 8th War Loan, is no exception. The green dragon, which represents the enemy, is shot through with seven arrows whilst it is throttled by the number 8, where the number represents the funds raised by the poster's financial initiative. War loans were securities issued by the government specifically to finance the cost of the fighting. Despite his contributions during World War One, Klinger suffered at the hands of the Nazis because of his Jewish descent and is assumed to have died after his deportation to Minsk in 1942.

The color palette row below is a sampler of colors selected from the *8. Kriegsanleihe* poster shown here, and is representative of the range of colors a designer working in this style might have used during the 1910s.

Although the **Plakatstil** style relies on simplification, shapes still take on dynamic form, as in the spiked fins of the dragon which help to add a sense of movement.

The large area of flat color forming the background of the poster with the main element centred within is typical of the Plakatstil manner of composition.

The large number 8 is used symbolically to throttle the enemy, represented by the green dragon which is shot through with arrows for good measure.

c =	000%	000%	025%	070%	090%	000%	010%	000%
m =	010%	020%	030%	025%	045%	085%	090%	000%
y =	020%	040%	045%	080%	090%	100%	100%	000%
k =	000%	000%	000%	040%	060%	000%	005%	100%

1920s

To many people the "Roaring Twenties" were all about having as much fun as possible. World War One was over and people wanted to forget about the hardships that it had wrought on society. In Britain—which had incurred debts equivalent to 136 percent of its gross national product—and indeed in the rest of Western Europe, times were not so good and prewar normality was not forthcoming. Unemployment figures were high, women were forced to cede their jobs to soldiers returning from the front, and cuts in public spending were crippling for ordinary working-class people.

Living standards gradually began to improve and it is fair to say that anything would have been better than the hardships and loss of the previous decade. In America things were rather different. A brief economic recession immediately after the war soon passed and the booming U.S. economy launched the age of consumerism. The automobile industry grew rapidly along with other areas of manufacturing; the world's first skyscrapers in the shape of the Art Deco architecture of the Chrysler Building and the Empire State Building were inaugurated; and despite prohibition, the American people were determined to have a good time. Outside of the cities, however, life was not so easy and more than 60 percent of rural America existed in a state of poverty.

In design terms, the manifestos that laid down the rules for the development of graphic style over the next fifty or sixty years were all written and launched during the 1920s. It was during this decade that Modernism in its many varied forms truly found its feet with Dada, Constructivism, De Stijl, and Art Deco all playing their part, and with institutions like the Bauhaus leaving an indelible mark on design style which endures to this day. Significantly (at least for those of us that work in the graphics industry), in 1922, William Addison Dwiggins, the American book

and type designer, first coined the term "graphic design" in an attempt to collectively describe all his professional activities which included book design, illustration, typography, and so on. It took another twenty years or so for the term to fall into common use as the replacement for the job title "commercial artist," but he had at least set the ball rolling. In that sense, whenever the term graphic design has been used in the pages of this book it has sometimes been used anachronistically; a common habit when discussing historical design style and practice.

Above Broom was a groundbreaking American arts magazine published between November 1921 and January 1924 by Harold Loeb and Alfred Kreymborg. This 1922 cover is a woodcut by Fernand Léger.

Right Merz magazine was produced by Kurt Schwitters from 1923 to 1932. This cover dates from April 1924 and was designed by El Lissitzky. *Collection Merrill C. Berman*

Above Eight Red Rectangles, *Kazimir Malevich, 1915.*

Constructivism

To understand Constructivism, or more specifically Russian Constructivism, one must first look briefly at Suprematism, a style devised around 1915 by the artist Kazimir Malevich. The name derives from Malevich's reference to "the supremacy of pure feeling in creative art." Based on Cubist abstraction techniques taken to the extreme, Suprematist paintings consist of solid blocks of color, often arranged in diagonal compositions designed to suggest dynamic movement. The style is strongly reminiscent of the Constructivist composition and typography soon to follow, and all the main Constructivist designers were influenced by it in some way.

Immediately after the 1917 revolution, the Soviet authorities' acceptance of artistic expression and avant-garde styles like Suprematism was initially enthusiastic, but this attitude soon changed to one of rejection of anything that could not claim to represent a practical use for the new socialist society. The sculptor Vladimir Tatlin and his friend Alexander Rodchenko (see pages 72–3) combined Suprematism with their own ideas for a more utilitarian or industrial form of art and in 1921 the term "Constructivism" was coined. Malevich had by this time taken a post at Marc Chagall's Vitebsk art school, where his Suprematist teachings had a profound effect on his colleague El Lissitzky (see page 53), who, like Rodchenko, was an ardent communist and supported the Bolshevik government's aims. El Lissitzky soon realized that Constructivism was better suited to serve the revolution and would, along with Rodchenko, become one of the main protagonists of the style during its early years. To help illustrate the practical nature of their style, Constructivists invented the term "Productivism." Russian graphic designers acquired an elevated status in Soviet society for a time because of their association with the revolution and the promotion of its status. This allowed them a little more freedom to express themselves politically and to assume the cultural roles previously fulfilled by artists.

Under the communist leader Vladimir Lenin's policies for the regeneration of Russian industry a number of private businesses were allowed to operate in competition with the State. A great deal of advertising work was generated as a result, and it is this period of activity that provides much of the body of work associated with the Russian Constructivists. The common message running through Russian advertising at this time provides us with a striking contrast to the techniques employed by graphic designers in the West. While European and American designers were striving to sell products or services using tried and tested methods of persuasion, Russian advertising relied on emotional techniques similar to

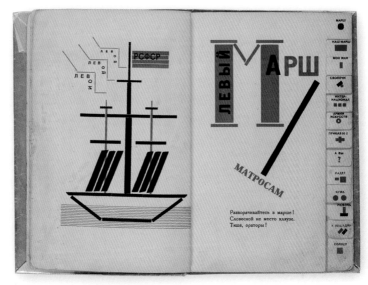

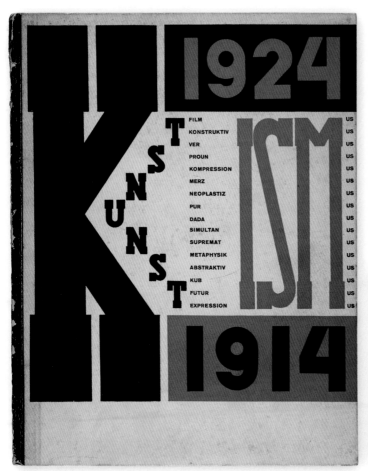

Above *El Lissitzky designed the cover and interior of* For the Voice, *a 1923 book of poetry by Vladimir Mayakovsky, using only the blocks found in a metal typecase.*

Left *El Lissitzky's 1924 design for* The Isms of Art, *co-edited with Dadaist Has Arp, set new standards of book design and layout that were hugely influential during the 1920s and beyond.*

Below *The Hungarian literary magazine* Ma (Today) *with a cover designed by Lajos Kassák in 1923.*
Collection Merrill C. Berman

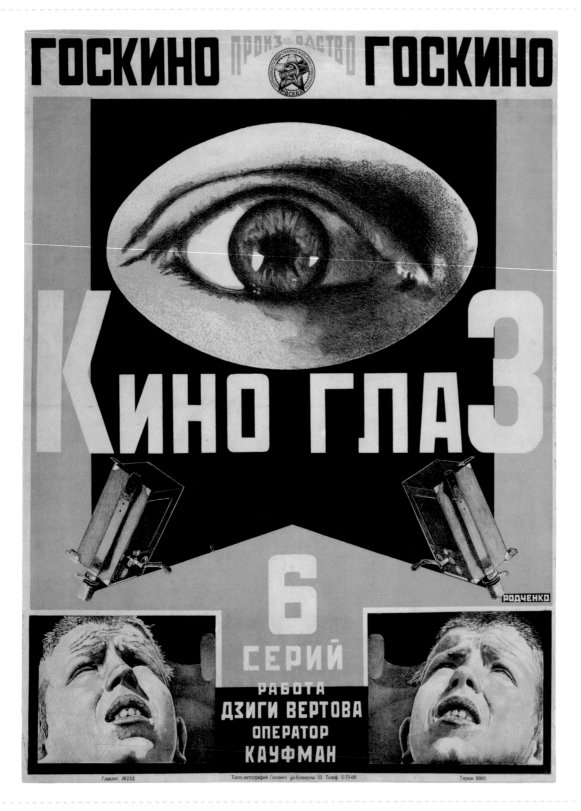

those employed in the propaganda and recruitment posters produced by the British during World War One. Patriotism—a duty to rise to the challenge posed by the aims of the socialist government—and an exhortation toward feelings of guilt if one had not given one's all were common themes. This link between advertising and propaganda helps explain why Constructivism can often feel somewhat militaristic in tone. In style terms, Constructivist artwork tends towards a certain visual sparsity; color is often limited to only two or three plates, with red and black a common and obvious combination, and a distinct lack of decoration serves as a retort to the bourgeois society the revolution had overthrown.

Despite the early acceptance of Constructivism as a positive force for the promotion of Soviet socialism, Russian Constructivist artists and designers often faced opposition from the authorities during the 1920s and early 1930s and particularly once Joseph Stalin seized power following the death of Lenin in 1924. Opposition eventually turned to outright oppression and in 1934, Socialist Realism was anointed as the official style that best represented the struggle of the working class and portrayed the leadership in a suitably heroic light. Many Constructivist artists and designers were forced to relocate to the West to avoid arrest despite their continued loyalty to Soviet ideology.

The style remained popular in the West, especially through the teachings of the Bauhaus (see pages 68–70) in Germany and International Constructivism continued as a major influence, primarily in architecture, for many years. A notable revival of Constructivist graphic design can be seen in the typography of Neville Brody (see pages 188–9) who drew inspiration from the style when designing custom typefaces and glyphs for use as headlines in the style magazine *The Face* during the 1980s.

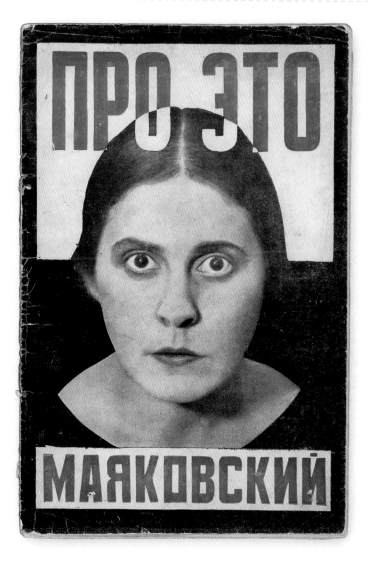

Opposite *A poster designed by Alexander Rodchenko for the 1924 film* Kino Glaz *(Cine Eye) which celebrated the achievements of a post-revolutionary Russia.* **Collection Merrill C. Berman**

Above *Another piece by Rodchenko, the cover of the 1923 book created in collaboration with Vladimir Mayakovsky titled* Pro Eto: Ei i Mne *(About This: To Her and To Me).* **Collection Merrill C. Berman**

Above *A Stenberg Brothers poster, designed in 1929, for the film* The Man with the Movie Camera. *Perhaps more than any other poster designed by them, this example demonstrates their masterful use of type and perspective.* **Collection Merrill C. Berman**

The Stenberg Brothers

Some of the finest film posters ever designed were created in 1920s Russia by Vladimir Stenberg (born 1899) and Georgii Stenberg (born 1900), brothers of mixed Swedish/Russian parentage based in Moscow. Their style combines Constructivism and Photomontage (a technique which involves cutting and combining two or more photographs together to create a composite image) with their own highly developed knack for perfectly capturing the essence of a film in a single poster. Compositions were dramatic, always full of dynamic movement and innovative use of typography, and their use of metaphor to pull story lines together into one image was masterful. Decent printing equipment in post-revolutionary Russia was hard to come by so the brothers designed and built a device which allowed them to project, distort, and copy individual frames from a movie by hand. Their posters appear to contain montaged photographic stills but the images are in fact hand-drawn lithographs. The projection technique gave the Stenbergs the freedom to manipulate images and typography in previously untried ways, and their use of mixed perspectives within one image was groundbreaking. Georgii was killed in a motorcycle accident at the age of 33, an event which Vladimir always maintained was orchestrated by the KGB because of their free-spirited lifestyle and their refusal to become naturalized Russian citizens. Despite this, Vladimir did eventually accept citizenship and continued to work as a graphic designer.

De Stijl

De Stijl (Dutch for "The Style") was founded in Leiden, The Netherlands, in 1917 with a philosophy which fused aspects of Cubism and Futurism with an extremely pared-back, pure aesthetic that is built around strong horizontal and vertical stresses. The painter and architect Theo van Doesburg had returned from service in the Dutch army during World War One nursing a strongly held belief that brutal nationalism and rampant cultural egotism had helped fuel the outbreak of the conflict. He wanted to promote a new culturally encompassing style with no direct links to any one country or society, and wrote, "The old is connected with the individual. The new is connected with the universal." As with other modern artistic movements, these somewhat utopian ideals were well meant but ultimately the De Stijl artists never truly achieved the universalism they sought and the movement's associations remained firmly Dutch. However, as a style De Stijl managed to make a significant and rapid impact on graphic designers and typographers while other postwar movements remained more firmly entrenched in the art world.

The movement was first brought to the attention of designers through van Doesburg's 1917 publication of *De Stijl* magazine, a journal which he continued to produce until his death in 1931. In line with the purist principles of De Stijl, the magazine was not over-styled and, from a graphic design viewpoint, was unremarkable. Certain covers, particularly the 1917 edition featuring a woodcut designed by Vilmos Huszár, were more illustrative of the De Stijl aesthetic. Van Doesburg would later go on to embrace Dada as an equally important revolutionary style and encouraged collaboration between designers and typographers working in either De Stijl or Dada. He died in Davos, Switzerland, from a heart attack after a bout of ill health. In terms of development, the style died with him but, similarly to Constructivism, it continued to influence graphic designers and architects for many afterwards years.

Above *A De Stijl magazine cover from 1926, following a template designed by Theo van Doesburg.*

Left *A 1926 piece designed by Herbert Bayer to promote an exhibition celebrating Kandinsky's 60th birthday. Drawing on De Stijl principles, the balanced use of the single image at top left and the type at the far right, set on a slightly angled grid, creates a wonderful see-saw movement which energizes the overall layout.*

The Bauhaus

On the April 12, 1919, the German architect Walter Gropius assumed his position as director of a new art school in Weimar, Germany. Formerly known as the Weimar Arts and Crafts School and closed in 1914 on the eve of World War One, *Das Staatliche Bauhaus* (which translates as "State Home for Building") was to become one of the most well-known and influential art schools of all time. From 1919 until its demise in 1933, its extraordinary complement of staff members and graduate students included many of the most important proponents of Modernism across every design discipline, from architecture and craft to graphic design and typography.

The school's ultimate aim was to reestablish a unity between the applied arts and technology to give design a fresh start after the stalling period represented by the war years. Architecture was central to the school's philosophy as Gropius believed it encompassed more distinct areas of art and design than any other discipline, but graphic design and typography were also key to student studies and competency in both areas was encouraged. The foundation year, led until 1923 by Johannes Itten, then afterwards by László Moholy-Nagy, was crucial for every student's development as it inducted them into the school's central message of "truth to materials" and taught them how to combine their ideas from different disciplines to create work which shared both visual and physical integrity. On completion of the preliminary course, students would go on to study in a variety of workshops which included wood and metal work, ceramics and weaving, and of course graphic design.

The Bauhaus' graphic design "style" is reflective of the early influence of De Stijl (see page 67), brought about in part by Theo van Doesburg's links with the school, and by Constructivism (see pages 62–5). Both design styles had emerged in the late 1910s and early 1920s, so were concurrent with the early development of the Bauhaus. Gropius himself was not in favor of perceiving any particular style as being associated with the school, but nonetheless typography in particular became heavily influenced by De Stijl. The poster designed by Joost Schmidt in 1923 for the now famous exhibition mounted by the school in the same year clearly demonstrates a move toward a cleaner, more technologically influenced aesthetic. Additional material in support of the exhibition was designed by Moholy-Nagy and student Herbert Bayer (see pages 74–5) who would later become a member of the teaching staff.

Above *Fritz Schleifer's 1923 poster for the Bauhaus Ausstellung (Bauhaus Exhibition) incorporates the Constructivist-influenced motif of a man's face in profile, originally created by Oskar Schlemmer in 1922.*
Collection Merrill C. Berman

Despite the huge success of the exhibition—which over fifteen thousand people attended—the relationship between the school and the Thuringian government of the Weimar Republic was not healthy. On December 26, 1924, the entire teaching staff resigned their positions, and by April 1925 the school and its students had moved to Dessau in the neighboring Federal State of Saxony-Anhalt where a new building—designed by Gropius—was completed in 1926. This was the most productive period for the school, which established The Bauhaus Corporation, an organization set up to transform original concepts created by the school into commercial projects. Ever efficient at self-publicity, the school published its own influential *Bauhaus* magazine, an excellent vehicle for the promotion of Bauhaus style. A series of fourteen books authored by such luminaries as Wassily Kandinsky, Paul Klee, Piet Mondrian, van Doesburg, Gropius, and Moholy-Nagy were also published. Bayer headed the typography and graphic design workshop during this period and established a firm influence over the cutting-edge graphics of the day.

1920s

By 1928, Gropius had resigned his post in order to return to architecture on a full-time basis. A number of staff changes followed, with the directorship going to architect Hannes Meyer from 1928 to 1930, and to Ludwig Mies van der Rohe for its final years. By 1931, the Nazis had become a powerful presence in Dessau and, after a series of intolerable cultural and political constraints was enforced on the school, it closed on August 10, 1933. As known intellectuals and under threat of persecution by the Nazis, many of the school's associates relocated to the U.S. and the New Bauhaus was established in Chicago by Moholy-Nagy in 1937. The school was subsequently renamed the Institute of Design and eventually became part the Illinois Institute of Technology.

Above *The cover of German journal* Offset Buch und Werbekunst, *designed by Joost Schmidt and published in 1926.* **Collection Merrill C. Berman**

The origins of Art Deco

The term Art Deco describes a style closely associated with the *Exposition Internationale des Arts Décoratifs et Industriels Modernes* (International Exposition of Modern Decorative and Industrial Arts). The event took the form of a world's fair and was held in Paris from April to October 1925. The architect Le Corbusier is credited with inventing the term itself when he used it in a series of articles published in his journal *L'Esprit nouveau* under the headline *1925 Expo: Arts Déco*. Art Deco, like Art Nouveau, is another example of a "total" style as it was applied to architecture, interiors, fashion, and product design as well as graphic design. It is essentially a more luxurious form of the earlier modernist styles and displays a noticeable Cubist influence as well as elements of Secessionist and De Stijl style. Art Deco is modern art transformed into fashionable lifestyle, representing extravagance, glamour, consumerism, and the glory of machine-age culture.

The origins of Art Deco can be traced back to the French decorative arts traditions of Art Nouveau. After the first Paris Expo of 1900, a hugely successful event that attracted thousands of visitors, it was felt that the French design industry had not made the best of that success. World War One clearly hampered further progress and a second Exposition for 1915 could not take place, but by 1925 things were back on track. The vanguard of Parisian retailers got behind the style for the Exposition, and major department stores such as Au Printemps and Galeries Lafayette represented themselves prominently at the show where they promoted the style and peddled their luxury products to the eager crowds.

Art Deco retains elements of Art Nouveau in terms of its penchant for ornamentation but is far less organic. The proclivity for curvilinear shapes is replaced by a harder geometry of intersecting rectilinear forms and precise curves. In graphic design terms, Art Deco represents quite a mix; the geometric forms so evident in Art Deco architecture are also

Above *A classic A. M. Cassandre poster from 1927 depicting the Nord Express train. The glamour of travel is inextricably linked to the Art Deco style and the power of the locomotive in this image is brilliantly rendered.* **Collection Merrill C. Berman**

Above *Heinz Schulz-Neudamm's famous and much mimicked 1926 poster for Fritz Lang's film* Metropolis.

present in graphics but the style of execution varies from designer to designer. In France, A. M. Cassandre (see pages 94–5) and Jean Carlu are considered to be the principal exponents of Art Deco, designing famous posters in the late 1920s and 1930s for shipping lines and railroad companies, department stores, and of course the wine-based aperitif Dubonnet. German designers such as Heinz Schulz-Neudamm, who designed the poster for Fritz Lang's film *Metropolis* in 1926, brought a more Futurist look to the table; and in America the style acquired its own name, Jazz Modern, and borrowed themes from Native American and Aztec art.

Alexander Rodchenko

Above *Rodchenko's cover for LEF (Left Front of the Arts) no. 3, published in 1923. Covers often carried a strong anti-czarist message.*

Of all the early Soviet-era graphic designers, the name Alexander Rodchenko conjures up the most vivid image of what we would describe today as classic Constructivist style. Born in St. Petersburg in 1891, Rodchenko moved to Kazan after the death of his father and attended art school there from 1910 to 1914 before continuing his education at the Stroganov Institute in Moscow. Initially a painter influenced strongly by Cubism, Futurism, and Suprematism, his career saw him move from art to design as his interest in the geometry of composition grew.

Like El Lissitzky (see page 53), Rodchenko was an impassioned supporter of the Soviet Communist Party. He joined Narkompros (People's Commissariat for Education) in 1918, and in 1920 the Bolshevik government appointed him Director of the Museum Bureau and Purchasing Fund, which was responsible for the administration of art schools and museums. In 1921 he joined the Productivists, a Russian movement dedicated to promoting art as a critical component in the process of industrial production, and indeed as an important facet of everyday life. This move prompted him to give up painting in order to concentrate fully on his work as a graphic designer, producing posters, books, and even films.

In 1923 he began a long collaboration with the Soviet poet Vladimir Mayakovsky, producing the creative arts magazine *LEF* (Left Front of the Arts), which championed Constructivist artists and utilized a design style based on strong horizontal and vertical forms; a design characteristic that would remain a prominent feature of his graphic output. He liked to combine these hard-edged compositions with images treated in the photomontage style of the Dadaist movement (see page 47), and it is this style combination which denotes his personal style as much as anything else.

It is not difficult to see just how much of an influence Rodchenko's work has had on graphic designers over the years. A prime example is the work of Neville Brody (see page 188–9) created during the 1980s, which indicates a great admiration for the Russian Constructivist style. Rodchenko's photomontage work, which often incorporated his own photographic images, also provides an extremely important point of reference for designers. His famous 1924 poster for the Soviet publisher Gosizdat

featuring his portrait of Lilya Brik shouting the word "Books" in bold Cyrillic has been imitated many times, particularly on record covers by British band Franz Ferdinand, who also used his 1923 poster *One-Sixth Part of the World* as the inspiration for their cover artwork. Rodchenko returned to painting in the late 1930s and died in Moscow in 1956.

Below *An iconic and much imitated image, Knigi (Books) was designed for the Soviet publisher Gosizdat in 1924. The woman featured in the photomontage element is Lilya Brik, the muse of poet and frequent Rodchenko collaborator Vladimir Mayakovsky.*

Herbert Bayer

Born in Austria in 1900, designer Herbert Bayer harbored a desire to become an artist from an early age. He originally planned to attend art school in Vienna but the unexpected death of his father meant that he instead became apprenticed to a local architectural and decorative arts studio under Georg Schmidthammer, providing an opportunity for him to cut his teeth as a graphic designer and draftsman. In 1920 he relocated to Darmstadt, Germany (as Peter Behrens (see page 36) had coincidentally done twenty years earlier), to work for architect Emanuel Margold before successfully applying for a place at the Weimar Bauhaus in 1921.

What he learned under the tutelage of the extraordinary roster of Bauhaus lecturers which included Walter Gropius, László Moholy-Nagy, and Wassily Kandinsky would inform his approach to design over his entire career. Bayer completely embraced the school's underlying philosophy that all design, first and foremost, had to be functional, and he was encouraged by his tutors to focus on his strongest area: graphic design and typography. He graduated in February 1925 and was immediately invited to take up a teaching post at the Bauhaus's new location in Dessau. In many ways his tenure as a Bauhaus tutor was an extension of his time as a student, as it allowed him more time to develop his skill set and to plan the establishment of his own commercial design practice. It was also during this period that he designed Universal, a sans-serif typeface which was adopted for use on all printed material published by the school.

Bayer moved on from the Bauhaus in 1928, relocating to Berlin where he was once again able to establish his own design practice. The opportunities Berlin offered were broader and Bayer soon found himself working on commissions for German *Vogue* magazine, and as a retained art director and graphic designer for the international advertising agency Dorland. He was able to incorporate much of his own Surrealist- and Dada-influenced photography into his work during this time and remained resolutely Modernist in his approach, a courageous stance considering Modernism was frowned upon by the National Socialists and was banned altogether when Hitler became Chancellor in 1933. However, by 1938 Bayer

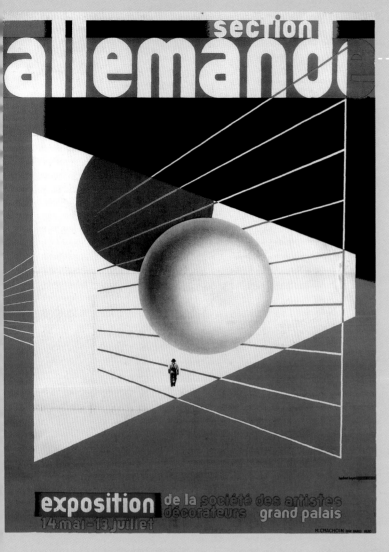

section
allemand
exposition de la société des artistes
décorateurs grand palais
14 mai - 13 juillet
M.CHACHOIN IMP. PARIS 1930

Opposite *Bayer's poster for the Europäisches Kunstgewerbe (European Arts and Crafts) exhibition staged in Leipzig in 1930.* **Collection Merrill C. Berman**

Left *A poster designed by Bayer for the Section Allemande of the German Werkbund Exhibition at the Paris Exposition de la Societe des Artistes Decorateurs (the Society of Artist-Decorators) in 1930.* **Collection Merrill C. Berman**

Below *Despite his Bauhaus pedigree, Bayer was capable of working in various illustrative styles as evidenced by the lithograph below. The piece dates from 1935, just before he relocated to the U.S.* **Collection Merrill C. Berman**

had had enough of a repressed Nazi Germany and moved to the U.S. where he continued to work on major graphic design and exhibition commissions, the first of which was the acclaimed Bauhaus 1919–1928 exhibition at the Museum of Modern Art in New York. His exporting of European modernist ideas into American design culture made him one of the first internationally recognized graphic designers. After a long spell living and working in Aspen, Colorado, he died in California in 1985.

The 1920s **075**

Jan Tschichold

Jan Tschichold's career spanned what many would regard as the most important decades of the twentieth century in design terms and his contribution to typography is hugely significant. Born in 1902 in Leipzig, Germany, he received a formal education in calligraphy and typography. This was unusual for the time, given that many of his contemporaries entered the design profession via a different route, be it via an art-based or architectural background. Studying at the Leipzig Academy for Graphic Arts and Book Trades from 1919 to 1923 provided him with a sound knowledge of the principles of classic typography, but he was profoundly affected by what he saw when attending the 1923 Bauhaus exhibition in Weimar and resolved to reject much of his acquired learning in favor of an approach fueled by his growing appreciation of the work of the Russian Constructivists. His early work utilizes pared-down geometric composition, sans-serif typefaces set in only upper- or lower-case, and photography favored above illustration.

He first published his ideas on typographic design in a 1925 edition of the trade journal *Typographische Mitteilungen*; an exhibition followed in 1927 and his most influential work, the book *Die Neue Typographie*, was published in 1928. The book, which he intended to be used as a handbook by designers and printers, was uncompromising in its advocacy for the use of Modernist typographic and layout principles. It covered everything from stationery design to advertisements and posters, newspapers, and complete book layouts, and became an instant classic which still influences graphic designers with Modernist sensibilities to this day. Despite the success of *Die Neue Typographie* and of several follow-up publications covering similar ground, Tschichold began to reject his Modernist ideals only a few years later and gradually moved back toward a more classical approach to typeface selection. Interestingly, his modest artisanal background (his father worked as a signwriter) helped set him apart from most other prolific typographers of his day in that he always used

GEORG JACOBYS WELTREISEFILM

PHOEBUS-PALAST
ANFANGSZEITEN: 4, 6¹⁵, 8⁰⁰   SONNTAGS: 1⁴⁵, 4, 6¹⁵ 8³⁰

ENTWURF: JAN TSCHICHOLD, PLANEGG B.MCH.   DRUCK: GEBR. OBPACHER AG. MÜNCHEN

Opposite *An exhibition poster designed by Tschichold for* Der Berufsphotograph *(The Professional Photographer) in 1938. This is one of the last pieces he designed using his new typography principles.* **Collection Merrill C. Berman**

Left *A film poster designed for the Phoebus-Palast cinema in Munich to promote the screening of* Die Frau ohne Namen, Zweiter Teil (The Woman Without a Name, part 2) *in 1927. In the lead-up to his book* Die Neue Typographie *he used sans-serif type exclusively.* **Collection Merrill C. Berman**

stock fonts from established foundries rather than custom hand-drawn letterforms. He eventually went so far as to state that *Die Neue Typographie* was too extreme, and condemned Modernist design as altogether too authoritarian.

In 1933, not long after Tschichold had taken a teaching post in Munich on the invitation of Paul Renner, he and his wife Edith were arrested by the Nazi authorities and accused of harboring communist sympathies. Fortunately they managed to execute an escape to Switzerland where Tschichold continued to teach and to work for the publisher Benno Schwabe. He went on to work for Penguin Books in England,

where he created the legendary Penguin Composition Rules which standardized the design of over 500 of their paperbacks, and during 1966 to 1967 created the beautiful typeface Sabon which was designed to reproduce identically on both Monotype and Linotype systems. Tschichold's legacy is that his consistently high standards helped draw the worlds of art, design, and typography closer together to help form the industry we know today. He died in Locarno, Switzerland, in 1974.

Bifur
Kabel
Futura
Bembo
Gill Sans
BREME
BROADWAY

Bauhaus * Fournier * Memphis * Memphis 7

In experimental terms, the 1920s are unequaled with regard to type design. The Bauhaus was central to the development of the new aesthetic, favoring geometric sans-serif faces, while the flamboyant movement known as Art Deco, which began to emerge toward the end of the decade, introduced highly decorative elements to type design with a focus on style rather than strict legibility.

Bremen
Richard Lipton (from lettering by Ludwig Hohlwein) | 1922

Fournier
Pierre Simon Fournier | 1742—Monotype Design Studio | 1924

Bauhaus
Herbert Bayer (based on his experimental font Universal) | 1925

Futura
Paul Renner | 1927–30

Kabel
Rudolf Koch | 1927–9

Broadway
Morris Fuller Benton | 1928

Gill Sans
Eric Gill | 1928–9

Bembo
Francesco Griffo | 1496—Monotype Design Studio | 1929

Bifur
A. M. Cassandre | 1929

Memphis
Rudolf Wolf | 1929

Bauhaus

ABCDEFGHIJKLM
NOPQRSTUVWXYZ
abcdefghijklm
nopqrstuvwxyz
1234567890
(.,:;?!$£&-*){ÀÓÜÇ}

The Bauhaus (see pages 68–70) embraced the use of rational geometric typefaces as part of its doctrine and experimented widely with typeface design. Sans-serif type was favored partly because it removed any associations with the nationalistic blackletter typefaces previously favored in Germany. In 1923 Herbert Bayer (see pages 74–75) began work on the design of an all-purpose typeface for use in all publications produced by the Bauhaus and drew several versions over the following years. His typeface consisted of strokes of a uniform thickness with characters composed of perfect circles and horizontal and vertical strokes. He called his typeface Universal and only drew the lowercase characters—Bauhaus is the modern version of the font, designed in 1975 by Ed Benguiat and Victor Caruso.

Futura

ABCDEFGHIJKLM
NOPQRSTUVWXYZ
abcdefghijklm
nopqrstuvwxyz
1234567890
(.,:;?!$£&-*){ÀÓÜÇ}

One of the best-known sans-serif typefaces of all time, Futura was designed in Germany by Paul Renner in 1927 and first released by the Bauersche Geisserei foundry in Frankfurt three years later in 1930. The typeface is particularly important because of the major role it played in shifting design sensibilities away from heavy gothics and blackletter typefaces that were so popular in post-World War One Germany— sans-serif typefaces established themselves as the fonts of choice for designers throughout Western Europe. At a glance Futura seems to be constructed of pure geometric shapes, and indeed the design process began as such, but over time subtle nuances in stroke widths and character proportions have improved the legibility of this timeless typeface which remains in extensive use today.

Gill Sans

ABCDEFGHIJKLM
NOPQRSTUVWXYZ
abcdefghijklm
nopqrstuvwxyz
1234567890
(.,:;?!$£&-*){ÀÓÜÇ}

Eric Gill's commission to design a new sans-serif typeface for Stanley Morison at Monotype came about after Morison spotted Gill's hand lettering on a store front in Bristol, England. He was looking for an answer to the flood of sans-serif typefaces emerging from Germany's type foundries at the time and saw it in Gill's elegantly proportioned characters. The first weights of the typeface were released in 1928 and the type family quickly grew to include bold, condensed, and display weights that could be used in projects ranging from train timetables to large signage. Gill's training (under calligrapher Edward Johnston, see page 57) provided him with the skills to create letter forms that were highly legible while managing to display a character all of their own, which helps to explain why the typeface still enjoys such immense popularity.

Bifur

ABCDEFGHIJKLM
NOPQRSTUVWXYZ
abcdefghijklm
nopqrstuvwxyz
1234567890
(.,:;?!£&-*){ÀÓÜÇ}

A. M. Cassandre (see pages 94–5) designed several typefaces during his career, the first being Bifur, which he drew for the Deberny & Peignot Foundry in 1929. It is arguably the most overtly Art Deco typeface ever designed, with its almost architectural geometry and highly stylized characteristics typical of the Art Deco style. Clearly the typeface is only suited for use as display or headline type for book titles or posters, and was only ever intended to be used in that way. It is so highly stylized that it fell out of fashionable use, alongside Art Deco itself. However, the character shapes, which display a certain elegance despite their sharp geometry, are extremely evocative and are the perfect choice for 1920s–30s design pastiche.

Gewerbliche Fachschulen Bayerns

Paul Renner | 1928

The lettering at the head of the poster resembles a condensed form of **Futura** with one or two slight differences, such as the angled terminals on the letter C.

The triangular shape created on the right side of the artwork is mirrored on the left, creating an overall balance to the composition of the poster.

The use of angled text and shapes is reminiscent of both **De Stijl** and **Bauhaus** style. Renner was not associated directly with the Bauhaus but shared the views of its tutors.

Although Paul Renner is best remembered as the designer of the highly versatile and ever popular Futura family of typefaces, he began design life as a painter but switched career paths after becoming involved with the Deutscher Werkbund (German Association of Craftsmen) in 1907. While working as a bookbinder he became increasingly involved in designing all aspects of the books, including the interior layouts and the choice of the typefaces for text and headline setting. As much as anyone else, Renner is responsible for the move away from the use of Gothic or Blackletter typefaces in Germany by encouraging the use of modern roman typefaces. Renner was profoundly interested in the relationship of form and function, as evidenced in his poster for the Gewerbliche Fachschulen Bayerns (Commercial Schools of Bavaria) designed in 1928, not long after Futura was finally released as a commercial typeface. The angled bars of type create balanced negative and positive areas within the composition, which is reminiscent of *De Stijl* and the Bauhaus style.

He was vociferous in his dislike for the anti-Semitic propaganda peddled by the National Socialists and suffered because of it; he was relieved of his teaching post in Munich and found it very difficult to find further regular work. Renner died in Hödingen, Germany in 1956.

The color palette row below is a sampler of colors selected from the *Gewerbliche Fachschulen Bayerns* poster shown here, and is representative of the range of colors a designer working in this style might have used during the 1920s.

Collection Merrill C. Berman

c =	005%	020%	035%	000%	000%	100%	035%	000%
m =	005%	025%	045%	025%	085%	080%	030%	000%
y =	020%	045%	075%	100%	100%	000%	030%	000%
k =	000%	005%	030%	000%	000%	030%	015%	100%

1930s

In 1929, Wall Street crashed and the financial reverberations radiated from the U.S. outward to create a financial crisis that would affect markets the world over. In America, what would become known as the Great Depression lasted for a decade or more, plunging international trade into a decline and pushing unemployment figures above 25 percent. Industrialized countries that relied on manufacturing for their national income were hit hard, and the farming industry was devastated by falling crop prices that dipped by over 60 percent.

This vast economic downturn fueled social unrest, making it easier for dictatorial regimes to seize power in Europe and South America. Despite this, the decade produced a flowering of new technologies, particularly in the fields of radio and film, and given the general state of the world economy it is somewhat surprising that Art Deco, as the style that epitomized luxury and consumerism, retained its dominance. Perhaps it ultimately came down to people looking for hope and an end to the misery of the times via the visual flamboyance of the style. Those better times were not yet to be: just as the Great Depression was drawing to a close, German troops crossed the border into Poland and the world was once again at war.

The prevalence of Art Deco

Art Deco style (see also pages 70–1) emerged in France following the International Exposition of Modern Decorative and Industrial Arts in 1925. Immensely popular during the second half of the 1920s, the style arguably came into its own during the 1930s when its "total" range of applications was fully realized. Aside from the thousands of products manufactured in the style—from china tea sets to coordinated suites of furniture—probably the most enduring example is the elegantly beautiful Chrysler

Building in New York. Completed in May 1930 after only two years of construction, it was the tallest building in the world until the Empire State Building was completed eleven months later, and is the epitome of 1930s style.

In the previous chapter, Art Deco was defined as a style celebrating the glory of machine-age culture. In that sense it is unsurprising that so many of the best-known pieces of Art Deco graphic design feature images of automobiles, trains, and ships. In 1935, A. M. Cassandre (see pages 94–5) designed one of his best-known Art Deco posters for the *Normandie*, a Transatlantic liner which was itself designed in the Art Deco style. The striking image of the ship's towering bow provides us with one of the clearest indications of the link between Art Deco, luxury, and glamour. A key element of A. M. Cassandre's work, and of Art Deco graphic style generally, is the seamless integration of image and type; the word *Normandie* placed directly below the bow of the ship to match the width of the hull draws the eye perfectly, making it impossible to separate the text from the illustration.

Art Deco retained its popularity throughout the 1930s but, following World War Two, the necessary austerity measures pushed all notions of opulence to one side. The style had, by then, also become more mass-market, which in turn offered a somewhat false image of the luxury it once represented, and it fell out of favor. A resurgence in popularity came with the publication in 1968 of historian Bevis Hillier's book *Art Deco of the 20s and 30s*, the first book to cover the topic in detail, and the style is often used today to evoke a sense of nostalgic glamour.

Above *Perhaps A. M. Cassandre's best-known poster, designed in 1935 to publicize the French Transatlantic liner* Normandie *which launched three years earlier. The ship itself became stranded in New York at the outbreak of World War Two and sank in the harbor after a fire broke out on board in 1942.*

Graphic design and the American magazine

American graphic design underwent a sea change during the 1930s. Previously, dominant design styles were conservative with little or no experimentation in evidence; Modernist styles had not yet made an impact on American design sensibilities. From the mid-1920s onward, a gradual stream of European graphic designers had started to relocate to America to look for opportunities to work in an environment less crowded with competing talent. This European exodus sped up considerably once Adolf Hitler became German chancellor in 1933.

All areas of graphic design benefited from the influx of fresh talent, but it was magazines that provided the best, and the highest-profile, opportunities for expatriate designers to gain commissions. The regular cycle of monthly magazine publishing provided a steady stream of potential work, and the obvious need for magazine covers to compete on the newsstand meant that exciting experimental work was more likely to be accepted. In 1929 the publisher Condé Nast hired Mehemed Fehmy Agha, then art director for the German edition of *Vogue*, to art-direct American *Vogue*, the culture and fashion magazine *Vanity Fair*, and *House & Garden*. One of the earliest changes Agha made typifies how impactful European design styles were to be on American graphic design. He began to use sans-serif typefaces such as Futura, designed in Germany by Paul Renner in 1927, and to fuse Constructivist design principles with Art Deco aesthetics. The result was a new style of magazine layout previously unseen in the U.S., bringing functionality and elegance together on the printed page.

Magazine covers were of course an important and highly visible vehicle to help designers propagate Modernist styles in the States. *Vanity Fair* covers regularly featured the

Below *This Harper's Bazaar cover from 1932 predates the arrival of Alexey Brodovitch in 1934 but already demonstrates the progressive nature of American magazine design of the period.*

FR · IN PARIS   50 CENTS   2/6 IN LONDON

Harper's Bazaar

MARCH 1932

COSMETICS
and TRAVEL

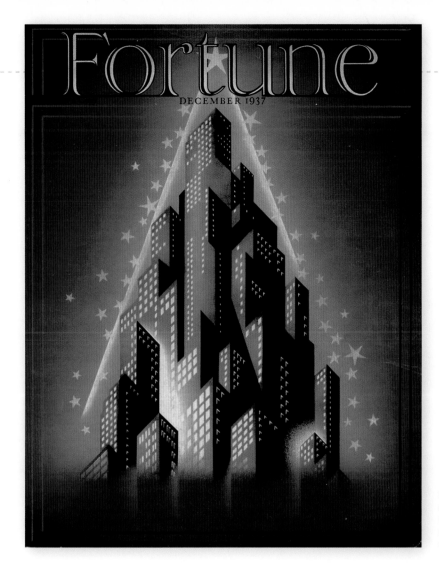

work of noted European and progressive American graphic designers, as did *Harper's Bazaar* and *Fortune*. *Harper's Bazaar* was art-directed by Alexey Brodovitch (see pages 114–15) from 1934 and was arguably even more progressive than the Condé Nast titles. Brodovitch hired the great A. M. Cassandre (see pages 94–5) to create a series of covers during 1937–39, and he himself designed some of the most eye-catching double-page spreads published at that time. Another famous Art-Deco-influenced cover appeared on *Fortune* in December 1937, featuring a skyscraper Christmas tree illustration by Austrian artist and designer Joseph Binder.

And it was not just the glossy lifestyle magazines that played their part. *PM Magazine*, a trade journal published by typesetting company The Composing Room, circulated widely among design professionals and featured work by European designers such as Lucian Bernhard (see pages 38–9), who had emigrated to the U.S. in 1923, and the enlightened American designer Lester Beall (see pages 116–17) who was one of the first non-European designers to embrace the principles of Constructivism.

1930s

Heroic and Socialist Realism

Heroic and Socialist Realism are not really autonomous styles in the same mold as Constructivism or De Stijl, and the terms can be seen as a way to describe art or design that falls under the umbrella of propaganda. Both approaches exhibit strong nationalistic overtones and a highly romanticized portrayal of political leadership or the working classes, and are dismissive of modernist styles, generally favoring a more traditional approach in terms of illustrative style. Heroic Realism emerged during the Russian revolution and was employed to propagate positive messages in support of the Bolshevik leadership. Lenin surmised that to convey information to a population with a high level of illiteracy, abstract imagery and avant-garde graphic design styles would not be understood effectively. Joseph Stalin was even less inclined towards a tolerance of Suprematism or Constructivism, and by 1934 Socialist Realism was chosen as the official style to represent the Soviet people's struggle. Constructivist designers were able, if careful, to continue to implement some modernist techniques in their work, but most converted to working in a style compatible with Socialist Realism. Poster production on a massive scale was used to educate the proletariat in almost every aspect of their duty to the new Socialist republic. Common themes included farming, manufacturing, and typical scenes of everyday life. Commissioned and produced by the State, much of the work was anonymously designed.

Around the same time in Nazi Germany, Adolf Hitler had come to power and modernist design styles were condemned as *Entartete Kunst* (German for "degenerate art"). Thousands of pieces of art and design classified as degenerate were seized from German museums, galleries, and private collections. In 1937 the authorities went so far as to organize a full-scale

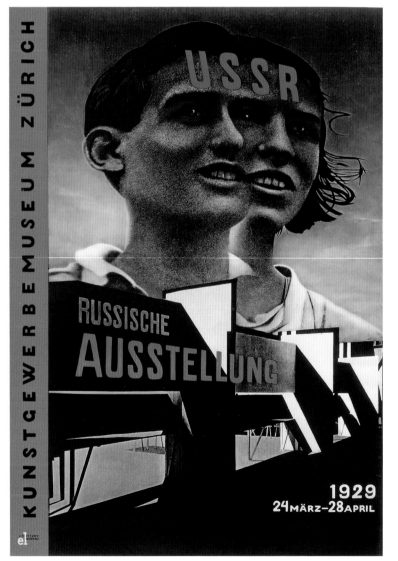

Left *Designed for a Russian exhibition held in Switzerland in 1929, this poster by El Lissitzky is clearly an early depiction of sexual equality, with the male and female figures joined and equal in status. Elements of Constructivist style are still evident at this stage.* **Collection Merrill C. Berman**

exhibition of degenerate art in Munich; it was assembled using work created in just about every style that had emerged since the 1900s and staged in a way deliberately intended to display the pieces in a bad light. The exhibition was also used as an opportunity to incite ill feelings toward Jews and after its run in Munich, the exhibition traveled to a further eleven cities in Germany and Austria. As mentioned previously, it was around this time that many graphic designers chose to leave Germany for the United States, heralding a new age of development for American graphic design.

Favoring seasoned poster designers such as Ludwig Hohlwein (see page 52), the Nazis preferred a classic form of Heroic Realism which portrayed the values of duty, devotion, and personal sacrifice in order to encourage intense feelings of nationalistic pride. Blackletter typefaces were also favored over modern sans-serif options. Though the effectiveness of the graphic design itself cannot be questioned (as we know, a large portion of the populations of prewar Germany and Austria embraced the message wholeheartedly), posters of this kind now come across as extremely stereotypical and idealized beyond all reason. It is also worth noting that the Nationalists in Spain used a form of Heroic Realism in support of their cause during the civil war and beyond.

Heroic and Socialist Realism still forms a powerful component of the propaganda used in support of governments in countries under the control of communist-backed military regimes, a prime example being North Korea. The same could once have been said of China but—after the death of Chairman Mao Zedong and the end of the Cultural Revolution, and as China has become increasingly westernized—the overall use of Socialist Realism has declined.

Above *Ludwig Hohlwein's 1934 poster* Reichssporttag des B.D.M. (*The Reich Sports Day of the Association of German Girls*) *is an arresting piece of design despite its unpleasant context, with the shape of the athlete's body mimicking the form of the swastika in the background.*

1930s

Pulp magazines

Of all the design styles which endure in some way or another, one stands out as much for its kitsch gaudiness as for anything else and is still frequently imitated—the Pulp magazine style. In fact, Pulp is responsible for creating some degree of "style confusion" in terms of where it is to be placed in twentieth century design history; people often identify the look as 1950s, but they are off the mark as its heyday can be traced to the late 1920s and 1930s, and more specifically to the years of the Great Depression.

Pulp magazines were not a new idea in the 1930s. They had been around in some form or another since the beginning of the century and are so called because they were printed on cheap paper stock made from wood pulp. The pulps were next-generation penny dreadfuls or dime magazines, the respective British and American terms for the short fiction magazines popular in the nineteenth century, and were marked by their distinctive cover art depicting the generally lurid stories they carried. Art Deco was the dominant graphic design style throughout the 1930s in America, and Constructivism was still popular, although its potency was waning in Europe, but pulp covers paid little attention to their influence. During the years of the Great Depression people were eager for any form of cheap escapism to take their minds off their troubles, and the most popular pulps could sell a million copies per issue.

Although covers occasionally featured photography, the vast majority of pulp covers were painted by illustrators in a representational style. The focus of each cover image obviously needed to have some connection, however tenuous in some cases, to the story line of the magazine, but the most important component had to be that they would be eye-catching enough to stand out from other magazines on a newsstand. Because of this, bold colors, crudely rendered hand-drawn typefaces, and

a great deal of visual innuendo were standard features, along with the almost ubiquitous, provocatively attired femme fatale. The covers eventually became such an important part of the sales process that they would sometimes by commissioned before the story; authors would be shown the cover art and asked to write text to match the image!

Covers were usually printed on better-quality paper stock than the interior pages, so could be produced with color lithography. The cheap paper stock was not capable of holding much detail, so illustrations for the interior of the magazine had to be black-line only without tonal shading or fine detail, and the style has been credited as a predecessor of the more modern comic book or graphic novel illustration style.

Above and opposite Spicy Mystery Stories *covers dating from October 1935 to August 1936.*

SPICY MYSTERY STORIES for FEB

BATMAN
by Lew Merrill

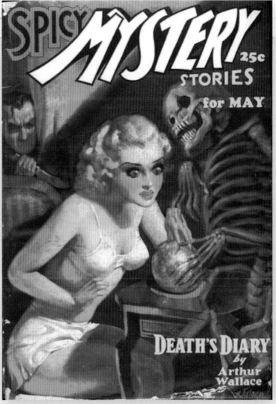

SPICY MYSTERY STORIES for MAY 25c

DEATH'S DIARY
by Arthur Wallace

SPICY MYSTERY STORIES for JUNE 25c

THE CAT TASTES BLOOD
by Gary Moran

SPICY MYSTERY STORIES for AUGUST 25c

THE EVIL FLAME
by Justin Case

Edward McKnight Kauffer

Above *The Art Deco influence in this 1930 poster for the London Underground is unmistakable.* **Collection Merrill C. Berman**

Opposite *Kauffer's 1932 poster for Aeroshell Lubricating Oil is a visual celebration of the speed and power of the automobile.* **Collection Merrill C. Berman**

Edward McKnight Kauffer, one of the twentieth century's most important designers, spent a large portion of his career as an American abroad. Born in Montana in 1890, Kauffer was living in San Francisco and attending art school evening classes when he took up an opportunity to study at the Art Institute of Chicago for a short spell. While there he visited the now-famous Armory Show, the first international exhibition of modern art to take place in America. He was hooked, resolved to travel to Paris to study, and was fortuitously offered sponsorship by a friend, Joseph McKnight, who admired his work and encouraged him to make the trip. Kauffer was so grateful he incorporated "McKnight" as part of his own name and used it for the rest of his life.

After first visiting Munich, where Kauffer was introduced to the work of Ludwig Hohlwein (see page 52), an experience which would inform many of his later poster designs, he arrived in Paris in 1913. He attended the Académie Moderne (the Modern Academy of Fine Arts) as he had hoped, but the outbreak of war in 1914 forced a move to England. Kauffer had originally planned to return to America but loved what he found in London, and he was soon introduced to Frank Pick (see page 50), the publicity manager for the London Underground. This was fortunate, as Britain was generally not well disposed to Kauffer's modernist approach which incorporated elements of both Cubism and Vorticism (see pages 45-46), and at that time Pick was one of only a few people with the vision to provide Kauffer with commissions. His early posters for the

Underground, painted in a Cubist-influenced style, were a hit and he went on to design over 140 posters for London Underground over the next twenty or so years. This work provided Kauffer with excellent exposure and gained him numerous other clients, one notable example being *The Daily Herald*, which commissioned the well-known *Soaring to Success! Daily Herald—the Early Bird* poster (see page 46) in 1919. Drawn in a Vorticist style, the illustration began life in 1916 as a woodcut but was refined for use as part of the poster design. The Shell-Mex and BP petroleum company was also a regular client, commissioning an extensive series of publicity posters by him during the 1930s.

Kauffer's work was not limited to posters. He was acquainted with many people in the publishing industry and designed numerous book jackets for Gerard Meynell of Westminster Press, Francis Meynell of the Nonesuch Press, and Faber. He also worked for the publisher Lund Humphries, becoming their first art director and sharing a studio and darkroom at their offices in Bedford Square with the photographer Man Ray. During his time in England, Kauffer developed a deep affection for the country and it was with some reluctance that he and his wife, Marion Dorn, returned to the U.S. in 1940, shortly after the outbreak of World War Two. Although better known in England, his reputation extended across the water and he enjoyed continued success working on publishing commissions and for large companies such as American Airlines. He died in New York in 1954.

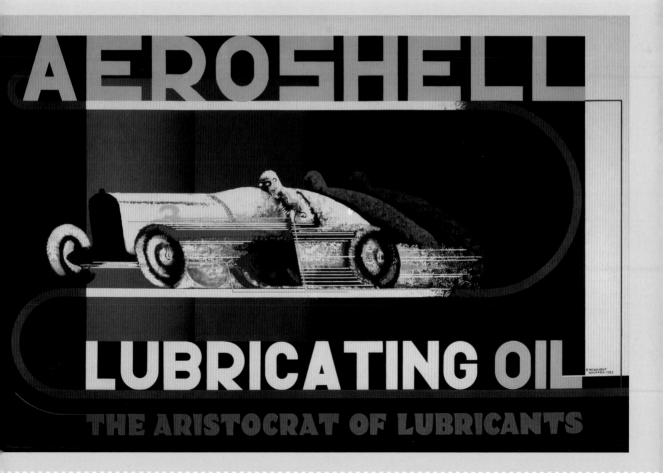

A. M. CASSANDRE

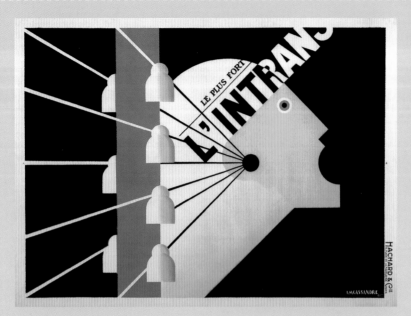

Although early influences included Cubism and Surrealism, Cassandre is generally regarded as one of the finest poster designers working in the Art Deco style which emerged in the mid-1920s and remained in vogue for the next twenty years or so. His earliest success came with a poster designed for the Parisian furniture store Au Bucheron (The Woodcutter) in 1923 which provided a clear marker for his subsequent output. The arrangement of the image anchored to a strong typographic foundation at the base of the poster was a recipe he would use time and time again to great effect—the ability to build up a composition by perfectly integrating image and type was one of his principal talents. Cassandre also exhibited successfully at the 1925 L'*Exposition Internationale des Arts Décoratifs et Industriels Modernes* (International Exposition of Modern Industrial and Decorative Arts), held in Paris, where his *Au Bucheron* poster won first prize.

A. M. Cassandre was the pseudonym of Adolphe Jean-Marie Mouron, born to French parents in the Ukraine in 1901. Cassandre trained as a painter at the École des Beaux-Arts and at the Académie Julian in Paris following the end of World War One and maintained a commitment to fine art throughout his life. Commercial opportunities for artists were on the increase as the dominance of the lithographic poster gave way to a broader range of graphic styles during the 1920s and 1930s, prompting him to begin a parallel career as a graphic designer. It was at this point that Cassandre adopted his nom de guerre as a means of separating his design career from his efforts as an artist.

Cassandre produced over two hundred posters during his career and many of his best designs were created for shipping lines and railroad companies. His monolithic posters for the transatlantic route plied by ocean liners such as *L'Atlantique* (1931) and *Normandie* (1935) are outstanding examples, as are his earlier posters for the *Étoile du Nord* and *Nord Express* train services (both 1927). His advertisement featuring the Dubonnet man enjoying several glasses of the alcoholic beverage is equally iconic and provided the company with what amounted to a corporate logo—the character quickly became indelibly associated with the brand. He was also commissioned to design several typefaces by Charles Peignot of the well known foundry Deberny & Peignot, who released the quintessential Art Deco headline typefaces Bifur (1929) and Acier Noir (1936), and the

Above *This early A. M. Cassandre poster from 1925, commissioned by the Paris newspaper* L'Intransigeant, *depicts the archetypal French heroine Marianne calling out the news of the day.* **Collection Merrill C. Berman**

multi-purpose Peignot (1937) which you can see used above in the heading of this profile spread.

Cassandre was honored with a solo exhibition of his work at the Museum of Modern Art in New York in 1936, and he subsequently spent some time in the U.S. working on cover designs for the magazines *Fortune* and *Harper's Bazaar*. He also worked for the advertising agencies Young & Rubicam, and N. W. Ayer & Son during this period. On his return to France he received few commissions so turned to theatre design, although he was asked to design the Yves Saint Laurent logo in 1963. Suffering from depression in his later years, Cassandre committed suicide in Paris in 1968.

Above *Dubonnet used the famous character created by A. M. Cassandre for this 1932 advertisement for over twenty years.* **Collection Merrill C. Berman**

Left *Cassandre's 1932 poster* Restaurez-vous au Wagon-Bar *(Restore Yourself in the Buffet Car) is a prime example of his ability to meld images and type together in perfect harmony.* **Collection Merrill C. Berman**

Herbert Matter

Above In what could be mistaken for an illustration at first glance, Matter's photographic montage for the Swiss National Tourist Office uses three layers to build the dizzying perspective into the image. The poster was designed in 1935 and issued in several different versions with various slogans.

Herbert Matter was another true all-rounder: a painter, graphic designer, and photographer who spent his professional life striving to forge links between fine and applied art. Born in 1907 in Engelberg, a Swiss mountain resort, Matter trained as a painter at the École des Beaux-Arts in Geneva before moving to Paris to study at the Académie Modern, during 1928 to 1929, where he was taught by Fernand Léger and Amédée Ozenfant. Here he was introduced to a style known as Purism, a variation on Cubism championed by Ozenfant and Le Corbusier, and used the idea of everyday objects placed abstractly in a number of his well-known poster designs. It was also around this time that his lifelong love of photography began to develop alongside his signature use of photograms (images created without a camera by placing objects directly onto the surface of photographic paper or film) and montage.

In 1929 he received his first break when the Parisian type foundry Deberny & Peignot, who were also the publishers of the influential graphic design journal *Arts et Métiers Graphiques*, hired him as in-house designer and photographer. During this time he was also fortunate to be given the opportunity to assist A. M. Cassandre (see pages 94–5) who periodically worked on typeface designs for the foundry during the late 20s and 30s. Matter was unfortunately expelled from France in 1932 for not having the correct papers, but his return to Switzerland ultimately proved to be a fortuitous event. He was approached by the Swiss National Tourist

Office and asked to design a series of posters
which would promote international tourism, a design
brief which Matter was born to fulfill. The concepts
he produced are strongly reminiscent of the
Constructivists penchant for placing a photograph
of a person staring out of the poster with bold, overlaid
typography at the base of the
composition. Matter combined his own
striking photography, which often
featured wildly exaggerated perspective,
with sharply angled type to create some
of the finest posters of their kind.

   In 1936, Matter took advantage
of an offer to travel to the U.S. as
payment for a project he had worked on
for a Swiss ballet company, and
subsequently decided to settle in New
York. A friend, who was aware that the
art director Alexey Brodovitch had
expressed an interest in Matter's
work, suggested that he make an
appointment at *Harper's Bazaar*, a
meeting which led to photographic
commissions for the magazine and
Saks Fifth Avenue, and established
Matter's reputation in America. In 1944
he became the design consultant for
high-end furniture manufacturer Knoll
and maintained their graphic identity
for over twelve years, designing
numerous promotional brochures and
catalogues. In his later years, Matter
became a design consultant for the
Guggenheim Museum and the Museum
of Fine Arts in Houston, and was
appointed professor of graphic design
and photography at Yale University. He
died in New York in 1984.

Below *Matter's trademark photomontage style
combined with the extremes of scale he often
employed inhabit this dynamic composition,
created for the Swiss National Tourist Office in 1936.*

Peignot

Monotype

Beton

Albe

Rock

*

Play

Schr

New Ca

Times New

Clarendon

rtus *

well

bill *

eidler

Joanna

edonia *

Roman

Despite the political unrest in Europe and the economic turmoil of the Great Depression, type design in the 1930s continued to develop at a pace to match the growing demand for printed communication. The clean geometry of modernism yielded slightly during this decade to accommodate the glamour of Art Deco, and the ever increasing use of typography as a primary design element began to sow the seeds of the International Typographic Style.

Joanna
Eric Gill | 1930–1

Times New Roman
Stanley Morison | 1931

Albertus
Berthold Wolpe | 1932–40

Rockwell
Monotype Design Studio | 1934

Monotype Clarendon
R. Besley & Co, The Fan Street Foundry | 1845
Monotype Design Studio | 1935

Beton
Heinrich Jost | 1936

Schneidler
F. H. Ernst Schneidler | 1936

Peignot
A. M. Cassandre | 1937

New Caledonia
William Addison Dwiggins | 1938

Playbill
Robert Harling | 1938

Times New Roman

ABCDEFGHIJKLM
NOPQRSTUVWXYZ
abcdefghijklm
nopqrstuvwxyz
1234567890
(.,:;?!$£&-*){ÀÓÜÇ}

Times New Roman lays credible claim to the title "most widely used text typeface in the world," which is probably true considering it is the default serif typeface on the majority of computer operating systems which use Roman characters. It was designed for British newspaper *The Times* in 1931, ostensibly to improve the quality and legibility of the text when printed on cheap newsprint, and debuted in 1932. The design was derived from Frank Hinman Pierpont's 1913 typeface Plantin and is attributed to two people: Stanley Morison, who at the time acted as typographic advisor to *The Times*, and Victor Lardent, who completed the final drawings. Morison generally gets the design credit but Lardent's contribution should not be underestimated. Because of its ubiquity the typeface is unfairly derided as dull in some circles.

Albertus

ABCDEFGHIJKLM
NOPQRSTUVWXYZ
abcdefghijklm
nopqrstuvwxyz
1234567890
(.,:;?!$£&-*){ÀÓÜÇ}

Albertus was one of the first typefaces designed by German-born designer Berthold Wolpe, an expatriate who spent most of his working life in England. Wolpe first trained as an engraver and went on to study calligraphy under the renowned designer Rudolf Koch at the Kunstgewerbeschule in Offenbach. His background shows through in the letterforms of Albertus which resemble characters cut into metal or wood with their flared glyphic serifs. The typeface was commissioned by Stanley Morison for Monotype in 1932 and began with titling capitals only—lower-case Roman and an italic weight were added over the following eight years. Albertus was extremely popular as a headline typeface during the 1930s and 1940s, particularly in Britain.

Rockwell

ABCDEFGHIJKLM
NOPQRSTUVWXYZ
abcdefghijklm
nopqrstuvwxyz
1234567890
(.,:;?!$£&-*){ÀÓÜÇ}

Rockwell falls into the classification slab serif (or Geometric Slab) and was designed by the in-house team at Monotype in 1934. The overall design was supervised by Frank Hinman Pierpont. Slab-serif typefaces feature serifs which are unbracketed, meaning the serif joins the stem of a character at a ninety-degree angle. Sometimes also referred to as Egyptians, slab serifs remained popular during the early half of the twentieth century before enjoying something of a resurgence in recent years. Rockwell is a fairly severe typeface with zero contrast in its strokes and is based on an older geometric slab, Litho Antique, which appeared in America in 1910. Other slab-serif typefaces of the time (for example Memphis, see page 79) are slightly softer in appearance but Rockwell still manages to exude a certain handmade quality of its own.

Peignot

ABCDEFGHIJKLM
NOPQRSTUVWXYZ
abcdefghijklm
nopqrstuvwxyz
1234567890
(.,:;?!$£&-*){ÀÓÜÇ}

Peignot is unusual among typefaces as it draws its influences from a combination of modern sans-serif and medieval calligraphy. A. M. Cassandre designed the typeface for Deberny & Peignot in 1937. Charles Peignot wanted a new typeface for the foundry which was both stylish and innovative, and Cassandre took his inspiration from the classic calligraphic styles used during the middle ages, mixing upper- and lower-case characters with extravagantly proportioned ascenders and descenders (the vertical strokes on a "b" or "p"). Further character is injected with the contrast between the thickest and thinnest strokes. Cleverly, Peignot was launched at the Paris World's Fair of 1937, acquired a reputation as the archetypal Parisian Art Deco typeface, and retained its popularity for well over thirty years.

Given that so many designers of this period came from an artistic background, it was considered perfectly normal for designers to **sign their work**. This is not a common practice for graphic designers working today.

The woman's hand is extremely stylized, so much so that if she were not holding a coffee cup to her lips it would not be obvious what the object represents. This actually encourages the viewer to look more closely at the image in order to analyze the content.

There is a hint of Schawinsky's more **precise style** in the overlaid linework depicting a container of coffee.

The hand-drawn typeface forming the word "Illy" is not a match to the company's usual script style logo but is used to emphasize the style of the painting. This is more or less unthinkable in today's market where guidelines for **logo usage** are followed to the letter in most cases, but in the 1930s adherence to corporate identities was not considered quite so essential.

Illy Caffè

Xanti Schawinsky | 1934

Alexander "Xanti" Schawinsky was one of the most colorful characters to attend the Bauhaus as a student during the 1920s and was known as the *enfant terrible* of the Bauhaus theatre. He was born in Switzerland to a Polish—Jewish family and enrolled at the Bauhaus in 1924 to study design and architecture, focusing on painting and photography during his time at the school alongside his theatrical exploits. Like several of his fellow students, Schawinsky would also return to the Bauhaus as a tutor for a time after his graduation.

By 1933 his Jewish origins were making life uncomfortable in Germany so he prudently relocated to Milan, Italy, where he stayed for three years, working at the well-known Studio Boggeri. During this time he produced a body of work which included commercial commissions for the Italian typewriter manufacturer Olivetti and the coffee company Illy. The style of the *Illy* poster is not typical of his usual technique which is more precise, but is likely to be painted in a style more reminiscent of Art Deco to meet the commercial brief, a fact which underlines his versatility as an artist. Schawinsky moved to the U.S. in 1936 and continued to produce innovative artistic and commercial work until his death in 1979.

The color palette row below is a sampler of colors selected from the *Illy Caffè* poster shown here, and is representative of the range of colors a designer working in this style might have used during the 1930s.

Collection Merrill C. Berman

c =	010%	005%	000%	010%	025%	040%	080%	090%
m =	005%	030%	060%	090%	085%	025%	080%	090%
y =	015%	020%	030%	070%	070%	020%	020%	030%
k =	000%	000%	000%	000%	025%	000%	010%	025%

1940s

British author H. G. Wells coined the phrase "the war to end war" in 1914 in reference to World War One, and in 1918 everyone clearly hoped he was correct. But Nazi Germany's invasion of Poland in 1939 put paid to those hopes and the world was plunged into another global conflict that would last until 1945. Economies were once again thrown into turmoil and the global nature of the 1939–45 conflict meant that it would take countries in Europe and Asia years to even begin to recover from the deprivations of wartime. Graphic design was generally circumscribed.

Technological innovation was limited to that developed in the interests of the war effort; large-scale warfare generally creates a spike in technological progress, which may mean medical breakthroughs or some other force for good rather than simply manufacturing better weapons. Jet propulsion and computing are two examples of technology that made great leaps forward during the course of World War Two. Though there was little progress in the development of printing technology or in the innovation of graphic styles during the actual years of the war, the decade did herald the beginnings of an American style of Modernism. This development was, in part, due to the number of European designers that had fled from Europe to escape political and racial persecution.

Opposite *Swiss designer Herbert Matter relocated to the U.S. after a visit in 1936 and produced a number of posters for various clients in support of the war effort. This poster from 1941 was commissioned by the Office for Emergency Management in Washington, D.C.*

Above *A wartime poster for the Office of Emergency Management by the great French designer Jean Carlu. Dating from 1941, the poster supports America's defense effort and is regarded as one of Carlu's best pieces.*

Mid-Century Modern

Following Adolf Hitler's rise to power in 1933 many graphic designers found it difficult to remain in an unstable and dangerous Germany which had once been at the very heart of the European design scene. Modernist styles had been suppressed by order of the Nazis and the work of designers working with Modernist influences had been declared degenerate. As a neutral country, Switzerland became an important centre for designers at this time and many relocated to either Zurich or Basel where the important art schools, publishing houses, and printers might offer work commissions or teaching positions. However, it was in the United States that much of the significant design development was to take place during the late 1930s through to the 1940s and beyond during a period known as Mid-Century Modern.

European expatriate designers working with a Modernist influence in the U.S. during the late 1930s were at times regarded by American designers as a little too bound to the rules of their chosen style. Their American counterparts tended to be more pragmatic and adopted a less rigorous approach to their graphic design work. New York at that time was probably the best place an ambitious and engaged designer could be, as one should bear in mind that the city's open-minded and egalitarian society and highly diverse racial mix was rich in alternative cultural influences. There was very little artistic baggage associated with American design prior to the mid-century period and personal expression was high on the list of graphic design priorities.

Of all the graphic designers that emerged during this period, it was Paul Rand (see pages 130–1) who did the most to promote a modern approach to American graphic design, and ultimately to champion the emerging International Typographic Style. His magazine covers of the late 1930s and 1940s changed the way American art directors approached editorial design, and his style would continue to influence generations of designers throughout his life. His book *Thoughts on Design*, published in 1947, is still considered a classic text on the subjects of typography and layout. Also, the work produced at George Nelson Associates Inc. for the furniture manufacturer Herman Miller from 1947 onwards by designers such as Irving Harper, George Tscherny, and Armin Hofmann was enormously influential throughout the 1940s and 1950s.

Above right and right *Irving Harper worked as a designer for George Nelson Associates in New York City for almost two decades, and during that time he created both the logo and a series of era-defining advertisements for the furniture company Herman Miller. The logo dates from 1947 and the magazine ad from 1948.*

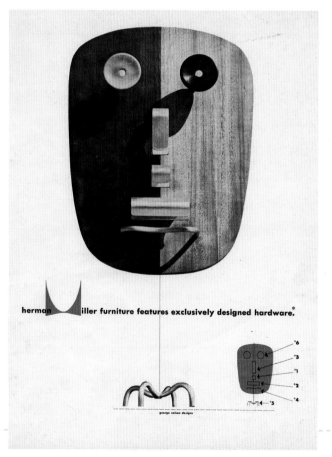

GROW IT YOURSELF

PLAN A FARM GARDEN NOW

Rural Electrification Administration, U. S. Department of Agriculture

Above *During the war years the U.S. Department of Agriculture matched the British effort to encourage the population to grow their own vegetables. This 1941 poster was designed by German designer Herbert Bayer.*

The Bauhaus goes to America

Walter Gropius left Germany for Britain in 1934, aided by the English architect Maxwell Fry, after duping the authorities into thinking he was attending an event in Italy. After a period working in Britain he emigrated to the U.S. and settled in Massachusetts in 1937, teaching at Harvard University on their graduate design program and filling the post of Chair of the Department of Architecture until his retirement in 1952. While there, he was joined by his Bauhaus colleague Marcel Breuer and the two men formed a partnership that would exert an important influence on many of their students, including well-known architects Philip Johnson, I. M. Pei, and Paul Rudolph.

Chicago saw the arrival of two more important teachers from the Bauhaus, László Moholy-Nagy and Ludwig Mies van der Rohe. Moholy-Nagy wanted to continue the work of the German school in a similar vein and despite some financial difficulties established the New Bauhaus in 1939. Herbert Bayer also moved to America around this time, settling in New York in 1938, but was not involved formally with the school. Sadly Moholy-Nagy died of leukemia in 1946, and the school was eventually absorbed into the Illinois Institute of Technology in 1949. Mies, who had been the final director of the German Bauhaus before it was closed by the Nazis in 1933, settled in Chicago in 1938 and became well known for his work on Modernist-influenced skyscrapers. Though all these men were architects rather than graphic designers, their highly visible work and their Modernist philosophy remain an important influence on the American design aesthetic.

Greetings from...

The inspiration for this book stems in part from a conversation about a style of linen postcard that was produced prolifically from the 1930s through the early 1950s. The design of the cards centered on snapshot views of North American States, cities and towns, and significant monuments, and more often than not included the words "Greetings from..." plus the name of the location in large three-dimensional lettering. The vibrantly colored postcards are called "linen style" because they were printed on paper stock with a very high rag content, meaning the cards looked and felt as though they were printed on fabric. Curt Teich of Chicago was the most prominent publisher of the postcards, along with Stanley Piltz in Sans Francisco, the Western Publishing and Novelty Company in Los Angeles, and the Tichnor Brothers in Boston. The printed cards were replaced in the late 1950s by glossy photographic prints, and original lithographic cards are now highly collectable.

Above *Printer Curt Teich emigrated to the U.S. from Germany in 1896 and based his business in Chicago. The company produced the distinctive "Greetings from..." postcards for over 70 years.*

Below *The company archive is now housed at the Lake County Discovery Museum in Wauconda, Illinois, and is the largest public collection of its kind in North America.*

UND DU?

HERAUSGEBER: DER STAHLHELM, BUND DER FRONTSOLDATEN   DRUCK: HERM·SONNTAG & CO, MÜNCHEN

Propaganda (part two)

In order to understand the stylistic approach to World War Two propaganda it is useful to first look at the way political publicity was created in Germany during the mid-to-late 1930s. Adolf Hitler wrote *Mein Kampf* during his period of imprisonment following his unsuccessful attempt to seize power in Munich in 1923. In it, he wrote that propaganda "should be popular and should adapt its intellectual level to the receptive ability of the least intellectual" citizens. We touched on this earlier in the book when discussing the poster styles of World War One (see page 48–9); Hitler is known to have admired the ruthlessness of British propaganda's central message and was dismissive of German propaganda from the 1914–18 war, deeming it overly decorative and ineffective. He was obsessed with symbolism and, as his power increased throughout the 1930s, the Nazi party began to commission posters featuring images of Germany portrayed as the master race. Ludwig Hohlwein was once again one of the graphic designers of choice—his style had evolved during the interwar years, moving away from Plakatstil (see pages 33–4) toward a brooding Art Deco-influenced look containing elements of heroic realism—and he created a number of posters in the years immediately prior to the outbreak of the war which carried a strong nationalistic message. Posters from this period clearly did their job in helping the Nazis to seize political power, but it is of course difficult to look on them today without feeling unnerved by our knowledge of their intention. The postwar reputations of designers like Hohlwein suffered badly as a result of their association with the Nazi party.

In Britain, because propaganda posters from the previous war had been criticized as too manipulative, much of the output became almost "undesigned." For example, recruitment posters were often a very straightforward proposition, carrying positive images of brave members of the armed forces, juxtaposed with uplifting phrases or quotes from Prime Minister Winston Churchill rather than wording designed to persuade action through a sense of obligation. Posters communicating issues related to civilian matters—"Grow Your Own Food" or "Women of Britain, Come into the Factories"—were generally more decorative or lighthearted in order to help boost morale, and anti-German posters often relied on black humor to get the message across.

In Russia, Constructivist styles had been suppressed by Joseph Stalin's Soviet regime and a return to an idealized naturalism, often referred to as Socialist Realism, had become the dominant style. In part, the move away from the more intellectually

We Can Do It!

WAR PRODUCTION CO-ORDINATING COMMITTEE

Opposite *This forbidding poster design by Ludwig Hohlwein actually dates from 1932 but is typical of the style adopted by Germany for much of its propaganda material throughout the 1930s and 1940s. The line "Und Du?" translates as "And You?".*

Left *Rosie the Riveter appears on this poster designed by J. Howard Miller in 1942. Interestingly, the character's name was applied retrospectively as it comes from a popular song written by Redd Evans and John Loeb a year after the poster was first produced.*

challenging work of the Constructivists (see pages 62–5) was designed to enable less well-educated rural citizens to clearly understand the message. Russian posters from this time generally feature images that are emotionally charged, designed to either boost national pride or generate anger and the desire for revenge.

Art Deco continued to dominate in the United States during the war years alongside a variety of traditional styles based around realistic representation, and both Art Deco and Constructivist styles featured heavily on American propaganda posters and literature. The continued popularity of Art Deco was due in part to the number of European graphic designers that had fled Nazi Germany and sought refuge in the U.S. in the years leading up to the conflict. In the early years of the war, posters showing support for Britain and its allies were dominant and emphasized how America's extensive production facilities were working in support of the war effort. Uncle Sam appeared once more, and the character Rosie the Riveter famously featured on a number of magazine covers and posters, including the *We Can Do It!* poster designed by illustrator J. Howard Miller in 1942.

Alvin Lustig

During his tragically short life, the American designer Alvin Lustig produced a body of work which defied the span of his career. He was born in Denver, Colorado, in 1915 and studied first at the Art Centre at Los Angeles City College, then as an intern under the great architect Frank Lloyd Wright at Taliesin East. This broad education meant Lustig alternated between graphic design, interior design, and architecture while residing on both the East and West Coasts in search of work opportunities, before starting his first design business at the rear of a Los Angeles drugstore when he was twenty-one.

It is important to note that when Lustig started out in the mid-1930s the International Style had not yet made its mark on American designers and Constructivism (see pages 62–5) had barely registered. As much as anyone else, Lustig helped shift U.S. design sensibilities away from realism towards a more graphically abstract approach. His book covers designed for Ward Ritchie Press between 1938 and 1940 display references to Vorticism (see pages 45-46) and Constructivism through the use of abstract geometry and ornament, and were quite unlike anything else being published in the U.S. at that time. Lustig was never afraid to challenge the perception of how a cover should function, and refused to accept that dumbing down would produce better sales for mass-market publications; he would often set titles in small discreet type and avoid any representative illustration in favor of symbolic imagery drawn from the book's content.

His work came to the attention of James Laughlin, the founder of New Directions Publishing in New York, who perceived Lustig's work as something approaching genius and began to commission book covers from him in 1941, beginning with *The Wisdom of the Heart* by Henry Miller. New Directions was (and indeed still is) a specialist literary book publisher, so Lustig's liberal use of symbolism in his designs received an extremely positive response from the readership. Lustig continued to receive regular cover commissions during the following fourteen years.

A lack of work opportunities took Lustig back to New York in 1944, where he became the visual research director for *Look* magazine and also began to channel his energies into interior design. On his return to Los Angeles in 1946 he opened an office specializing in furniture and fabric design while continuing to work on graphic design projects,

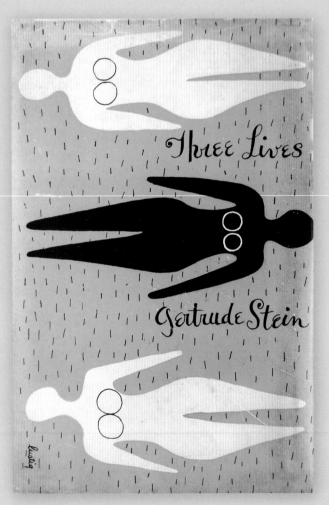

Left *Lustig's 1945 cover for* Three Lives *by Gertrude Stein, designed for publisher New Directions as part of their New Classics series.*

demonstrating his ability to move between design disciplines with relative ease. At the invitation of artist and teacher Josef Albers, Lustig also taught at Black Mountain College in North Carolina and at the design department at Yale.

Lustig suffered from diabetes as a child and by 1954 his sight had deteriorated to the point where he was virtually blind. He subsequently developed the incurable kidney disease Kimmelstiel–Wilson syndrome and died from complications in 1955, aged just forty. His wife Elaine, also a graphic designer, successfully continued his work after his death.

Left *Lustig's 1946 cover for* Fortune *magazine is a fine example of the way his occasionally idiosyncratic approach manages to bind a design together using a combination of abstract elements.*

Below *A spread from* Staff, *an in-house publication for* Look *magazine, designed in 1944.*

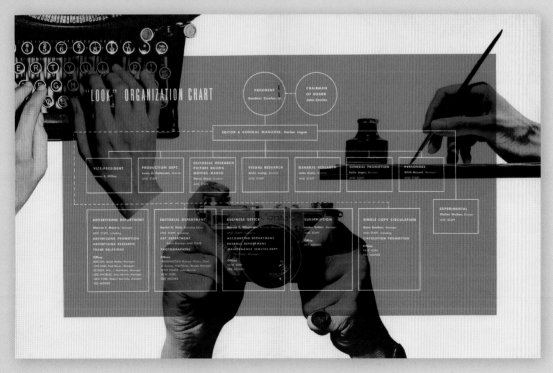

Alexey Brodovitch

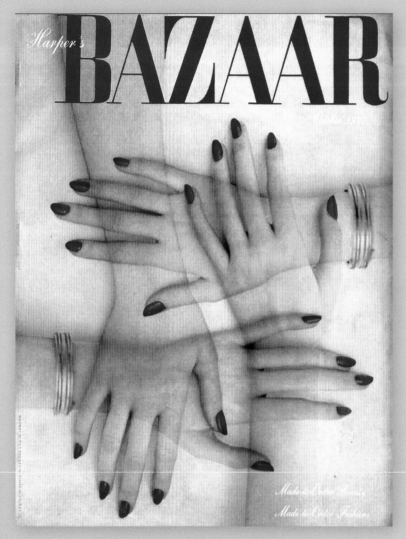

1920s Paris where he worked as a set designer for the *Ballets Russes* and as a designer for the magazine *Arts et Métiers Graphiques*. He had fought on the side of the Czarist forces against the Bolsheviks but their defeat compelled him to flee Russia. Paris's 1925 *L'Exposition Internationale des Arts Décoratifs et Industriels Modernes* (International Exposition of Modern Industrial and Decorative Arts) saw him win several medals for his fabric and jewelry designs and his career prospered, but he was nonetheless drawn to the U.S. in 1930 after being invited to establish a department of advertising design at the Philadelphia College of Art. He was instrumental in introducing a broad range of European design sensibilities to his American students and stayed with the school until 1938.

While still teaching, he took freelance commissions from clients in Philadelphia and New York and his work came to the attention of Carmel Snow, the new editor of *Harper's Bazaar*. She hired him as art director in 1934 and over the next quarter of a century his pioneering work would set the bar for fashion and lifestyle magazine publishing. Over the years he refined the way layouts were assembled and moved away from densely populated spreads to a more elegant form that incorporated white space as an element of the design and often eschewed the constraints of a grid. Brodovitch can arguably be cited as the template for all successful magazine art directors that followed him. He would involve himself in all aspects of production, conceive and commission all visual content for each edition, and he introduced the work of many well-known figures from the European art and

Alexey Brodovitch was born in Russia in 1898 and is regarded as one of the foremost magazine art directors of his generation. The development of graphic design from the 1930s through to the 1950s is closely linked to the blossoming of a new form of visual language, particularly in the U.S. where the public had not been exposed to as many radical design styles as the people of Europe, and magazines provided the ideal platform to showcase the emerging talents of graphic designers, illustrators, and photographers.

It is for his tenure at *Harper's Bazaar* from 1934 to 1958 that he is best known, but his career began in

design world to the U.S. audience. The artists Man Ray, A. M. Cassandre, and Salvador Dalí were all commissioned, as were the photographers Bill Brandt, Brassaï, Herbert Matter, and Henri Cartier-Bresson. He also worked with many up-and-coming talents and was among the first to hand out assignments to photographers Lisette Model, André Kertész, Irving Penn (whom he had taught in Philadelphia), and Richard Avedon.

Brodovitch was also responsible for the design of the hugely influential design quarterly *Portfolio* which featured transparent pages, die-cuts, and fold-outs, the cost of which contributed to its demise after only three issues in 1951. Despite this, the magazine is considered an important benchmark in the history of magazine publishing. He left *Harper's Bazaar* in 1958 and continued to work on freelance projects and to teach. He died in Le Thor, France, in 1971.

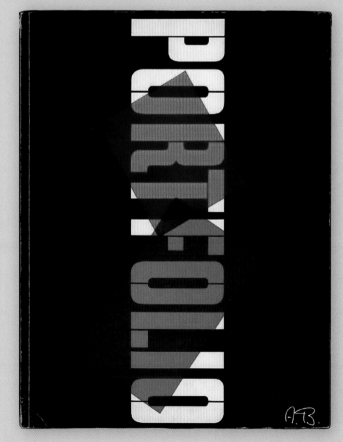

Lester Beall

Lester Beall was born in Kansas City, Missouri, in 1903 and studied at Chicago's Art Institute and at the University of Chicago before graduating and setting up his own freelance studio in 1927. He is remembered principally for the three series of posters he created for America's Rural Electrification Administration, set up as part of President Roosevelt's "New Deal" domestic reform programs; and as part of the new generation of business-minded practitioners he did much to help educate the commercial world in their understanding of how professional graphic design could help enhance a company's image and grow their business. Beall stated that the designer "must work with one goal in mind—to integrate the elements in such a manner that they will combine to produce a result that will convey not merely a static commercial message, but an emotional reaction as well. If we can produce the kind of art which harnesses the power of the human instinct for that harmony of form, beauty, and cleanness that seems inevitable when you see it, then I think we may be doing a job for our clients."

Relocating from Chicago to New York in 1935, Beall split his time between the city and his rural home in Wilton, Connecticut, where much of his well-known work was designed. His diverse client roster during the 1930s and 1940s included the Chicago Tribune, Hiram Walker, Time magazine, and the Crowell Publishing Company, which published Colliers magazine. Two covers designed for Colliers in the run-up to World War Two, "Will There Be War" and "Hitler's Nightmare," are considered classics and perfectly represent the style favored by many American graphic designers in the late 1930s. It was during this period that he designed the Rural Electrification Administration posters, working on three separate series between 1937 and 1941. The brief required Beall to create visual enticements for Americans living in more remote locations to electrify their homes, and the posters had to carry a clear message that could be easily understood by a rural population that was often low in literacy skills. Series one featured only graphic elements indicating how consumers could enjoy the benefits of things such as lighting, radio, and pumped running water, life-changing services for farming families struggling to mechanize. Series two added photomontage layouts featuring portraits of consumers and positive slogans; and series three prominently featured nationalistic red, white, and blue elements to emphasize the "we're in this together" nature of the project.

By the 1950s Beall decided to unify his offices at one location, Dumbarton Farm in Brookfield, Connecticut, and spent much of his time on corporate identity projects for clients such as Merrill Lynch, the Caterpillar Inc. tractor company, the New York Hilton, and the International Paper Company, for which he produced one of the first modern examples of a graphics standards manual. He continued to live and work at Dumbarton Farm until his death in 1969.

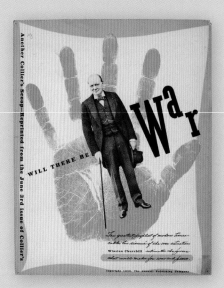

Above The Will There Be War cover of Colliers magazine, 1939. *Collection Merrill C. Berman*

Opposite Light, one of a series of posters created by Beall for the Rural Electrification Administration between 1937 and 1941. The simple but strong graphic messages targeted a rural population with potentially low literacy skills. *Collection Merrill C. Berman*

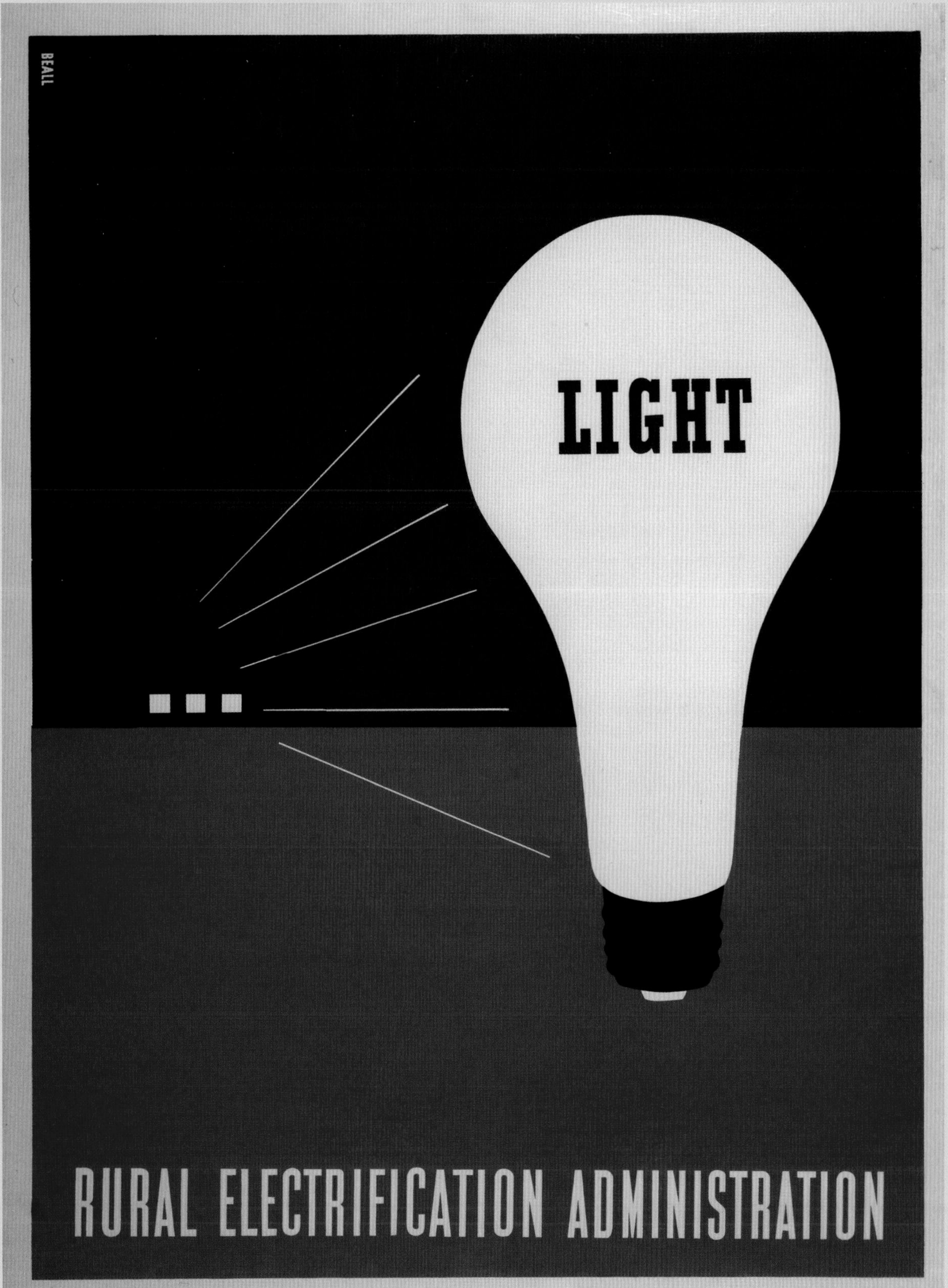
BEALL
LIGHT
RURAL ELECTRIFICATION ADMINISTRATION

american uncial

Brush Script

TRADE GOTHIC BOLD CONDENSED NO.20

Figaro ✴

CHEVALIER

Trade Gothic

The 1940s witnessed a downturn in the pace of development within the graphics and printing industries. World War Two absorbed the commercial and technological resources which would otherwise have been channeled into industrial development and it would be a number of years after the cessation of the war before any new typefaces could be designed and produced.

Figaro
Monotype Design Studio | 1940

Brush Script
Robert E. Smith | 1942

American Uncial
Victor Hammer | 1943

Chevalier
Emil A. Neukomm | 1946

Trade Gothic
Jackson Burke | 1948–60

Trade Gothic Bold Condensed No. 20
Jackson Burke | 1948–60

Key typefaces

Brush Script

ABCDEFGHIJKLM
NOPQRSTUVWXYZ
abcdefghijklm
nopqrstuvwxyz
1234567890
(.,:;?!$£&-*){ÀÓÜÇ}

Although Brush Script tends to appear in many ill-advised situations these days due to its inclusion in popular software applications, it does not fully deserve its poor reputation. Designed in 1942 by Robert E. Smith for American Type Founders, the font is an early example of a casual script which makes a decent job of emulating handwritten calligraphic signwriting. There have certainly been many script typefaces drawn since Brush Script that are far less successful. The typeface was an immediate hit on launch and appeared in thousands of advertisements during the 1940s and 1950s, prevailing until the influence of the International Typographic Style (see pages 122–127) took a firm hold. It has regained some of its popularity these days, if only for its usefulness as a tool for ironic nods to the post-World War Two era.

Trade Gothic

ABCDEFGHIJKLM
NOPQRSTUVWXYZ
abcdefghijklm
nopqrstuvwxyz
1234567890
(.,:;?!$£&-*){ÀÓÜÇ}

Trade Gothic was designed by Jackson Burke in 1948, just before he began his tenure as director of type development for Linotype in the U.S.A. Burke's long-standing employment with the company (he was with Linotype until 1960) enabled him to expand the Trade Gothic family into an eventual fourteen-style collection which included three weights and three widths. As a family, it feels less unified than other similar typefaces such as Helvetica or Univers (see page 126), but this is not a negative as the different widths were really intended for different uses. For example, Trade Gothic Bold Condensed No. 20 has a flat-sided "O," "G," "Q," and so on, unlike the rest of the family, but this means it can used to make extremely powerful close-set headlines.

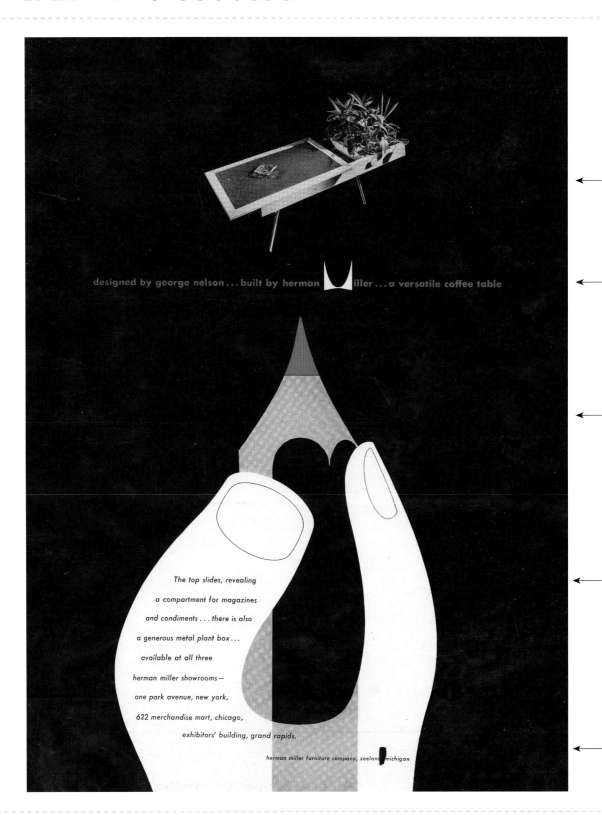

designed by george nelson...built by herman miller...a versatile coffee table

The top slides, revealing
a compartment for magazines
and condiments . . . there is also
a generous metal plant box...
available at all three
herman miller showrooms—
one park avenue, new york,
622 merchandise mart, chicago,
exhibitors' building, grand rapids.

herman miller furniture company, zeeland, michigan

Herman Miller advertising

Irving Harper | 1949

If there is one style of magazine advertising that personifies the cooler side of the 1940s marketplace, a strong contender has to be the work commissioned by George Nelson Associates Inc. for Michigan-based furniture company Herman Miller. Irving Harper joined the company in 1947 after he was offered a job as an interior designer, having worked previously for Raymond Loewy Associates in a similar capacity. Harper never received any formal graphic design training but was tasked with designing the trade advertising for Herman Miller. He subsequently created a logo based on a highly stylized "M" which became the company's corporate identity and is still in use today, albeit in a modified form. He has since joked that it is the cheapest logo design in history as there was no specific brief to come up with the identity, it simply came with the ad and was adopted almost immediately.

The 1949 magazine advertisement shown here, promoting a coffee table designed at George Nelson Associates and manufactured by Herman Miller, is a classic example of the look that designers today would reference when attempting to recapture the modernist styling of the 1940s and 1950s. The color palette row below is a sampler of colors selected from the advertisement, plus some supplementary colors, and is representative of the range of colors a designer working in this style might have used.

Photomontage was often used to represent the product in Irving Harper's ad designs.

Harper used the geometric sans-serif typeface **Futura**, designed by Paul Renner in 1927, for all trade advertisements designed during this period.

The inclusion of the pencil neatly emphasizes the design aspect of the product. As a company, Herman Miller's design standards were, and still are, particularly high and this is directly reflected in the graphic quality of the trade advertising.

The almost sculptural form of the hand is perfect for a piece of graphic design promoting a furniture manufacturer. The elegantly curved typesetting further enhances the sense of quality and style.

c =	005%	010%	000%	025%	045%	040%	075%	000%
m =	010%	080%	095%	030%	035%	045%	055%	000%
y =	005%	090%	095%	055%	030%	040%	035%	000%
k =	000%	000%	000%	010%	015%	025%	020%	100%

1950s

Despite the cessation of World War Two five years earlier, the 1950s were dominated by conflict. Communism and capitalism went head-to-head during a decade which saw the escalation of the Korean war, and later the war in Vietnam, and in the U.S. anti-communist sentiments ran high. The 1950s is also the decade that gave the world rock and roll, so it was not all bad news, while television first began to emerge as the entertainment medium of choice in America and in other westernized countries. Graphic design embraced and battled with materialism.

TV sets were still expensive, but by the end of the decade approximately 90 percent of American households owned one. Advertising was piped into homes via the box in the corner alongside programs filled with racial and gender stereotypes which idealized the western consumerist lifestyle, and it is perhaps because of this that the 1950s are seen as a decade of social conformity. In opposition, however, the influence of the group of writers known as the Beat Generation would have a long-term effect on style, drug culture, sexual liberty, and attitudes towards materialism; all issues that would continue to play a big role in youth culture in the 1960s.

The International Typographic Style

The 1950s saw the full emergence of a design movement that is arguably the most important graphic design style of the twentieth century in terms of its far-reaching impact, its longevity, and its range of practical applications. The style began in Switzerland and Germany and is sometimes referred to as Swiss Style, but it is formally known as the International Typographic Style. Its dominance in many areas of graphic design covers a twenty-year period from the early 1950s to the late 1960s, but it remains an important influence to this day. There are a range of

LIVING ROOM WITH T/V

Sideboard, cabinet in background, and pottery, etc., from Dunn's of Bromley.

Banbury Carpet. Design "Marble"—multi-coloured effects on rich grounds. Made by I. & C. Steele & Co., The Carpet Mill, Bloxham, Banbury. Obtainable from stockists of Banbury Carpets. **Cole's Wallpaper**—"Italian Tile" in special colouring on a marbled ground to match the scheme. Price 28/- per piece + ⅓th. Available in any colouring and on plain ground. **H.K. Furniture.** "Caramba" chair in foreground from £25/7/6. "Calypso" in background from £22/10/0. Two and three-seater settees to match. An unusually varied range of covers available on all H.K. Furniture. At leading shops. **Deep Textures** by Tibor Ltd., Stratford-on-Avon. Carpet and textures designed by Tibor Reich, F.S.I.A. "Cymbeline" curtains in Persimmon, with non-tarnishing metallic yarn, available at Liberty's, Regent Street. "Shaftesbury" in Cerulean blue on H.K. Furniture. **Pye 14in. Automatic Picture Control TV Receiver.** Apart from the elegance of the cabinet, the new invention—Automatic Picture Control—eliminates picture fading and picture flutter. This new feature was pioneered by Pye Ltd. **Troughton & Young Lighting**—Table and Wall Fittings F.1031, off-white shade, satin brass metalwork. Counter-balanced for use as table or wall lamp as illustrated in this photograph.

specific visual hallmarks that characterize the style. These include the use of asymmetrical layouts built around a mathematically constructed grid; a clear and unadorned approach to the presentation of content; the use of sans-serif type, generally set flush-left and ragged-right; and a preference for photography over illustration.

It is useful to place the development of the style in historical context as its early influences stretch back over several decades. In 1918, Ernst Keller—considered by many as the forerunner of the International Typographic Style—began to teach design and typography at the School of Applied Arts in Zurich. He never encouraged students to adopt a specific style, but he did argue that a design solution should always be respectful of content. This can be seen as an early version of the Modernist principle of form following function.

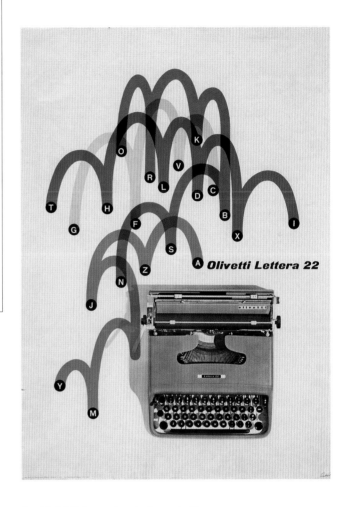

Above left *A British magazine advertisement of the 1950s which personifies the kitsch styling that is sometimes associated with the decade.*

Above *A 1953 advertisement designed by Giovanni Pintori for the classic Lettera 22 typewriter manufactured by Italian firm Olivetti.*

bergamo   s.agostino

1°
gran premio

bergamo

internazionale
del film d'arte
e sull'arte

8–14 settembre   1958

Above *Max Huber's poster for the inaugural international art film festival held in Bergamo, Italy, in 1958 demonstrates his trademark flair for exuberant color combined with Swiss Style typography.*
Collection Merrill C. Berman

Right *Huber's graphic poster for the United Nations Educational, Scientific and Cultural Organization, created in 1950.*
Collection Merrill C. Berman

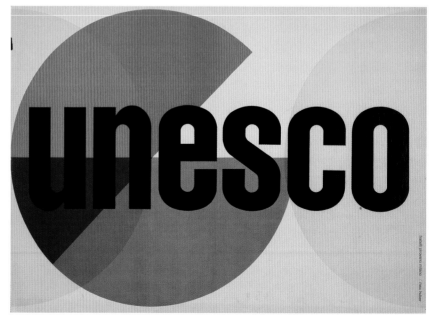

unesco

Over the following three decades, a number of important Swiss designers would contribute to the development of the style. Theo Ballmer studied at the Dessau Bauhaus (see pages 68-70) in the late 1920s under Walter Gropius and applied De Stijl principles to much of his graphic design work which utilized grids of horizontally and vertically aligned elements. Max Bill—another student at the Dessau Bauhaus from 1927 to 1929 where he was taught by Gropius, László Moholy-Nagy, and Wassily Kandinsky—developed a concept he called *art concret* which involved the creation of a universal style based on mathematical principles. His graphic design work featured layouts where elements were precisely distributed and spaced; he favored sans-serif typefaces such as Akzidenz Grotesk, and set text flush-left and ragged-right. On a more flamboyant note the designer Max Huber added a generous dash of energetic verve to the mix. Huber studied at the Zurich School of Arts and Crafts where he experimented extensively with photomontage techniques and in the late 1940s began to create some of the most exuberant posters seen at that time. He was the master of the layered composition, making use of overprinted shapes and dynamically positioned typography and photomontage to create work which includes his noted pieces promoting races at the Autodromo Nazionale Monza (National Racetrack of Monza.)

The style's total dominance throughout the 1950s is largely represented by the work of one central figure, Josef Müller-Brockmann, whose body of work is synonymous with the period. Müller-Brockmann studied under Ernst Keller in Zurich between 1932 and 1934 before opening his own studio in 1936. He was something of a convert to the International Typographic Style as his influences variously included Constructivism, De Stijl, Suprematism, and the teachings of the Bauhaus, but Müller-Brockmann managed to filter elements of all of these into his very particular and highly representative version of the style. Some of his best-known work was

Above *One of a series of road safety posters designed in 1953 by Josef Müller-Brockmann for the Swiss Automobile Club. The posters were produced in both French and German to accommodate the different languages spoken throughout Switzerland.*

commissioned by Zurich Town Hall from 1952 onward; he was asked to design a series of concert posters and devised an abstract visual method to represent the music using mathematically harmonious compositions. Another significant series of poster commissions came from the Swiss Automobile Club following their concerns about the large increase in the number of vehicles on Swiss roads and the issues that arose from that. His 1953 poster promoting child safety stands out as one of his best pieces.

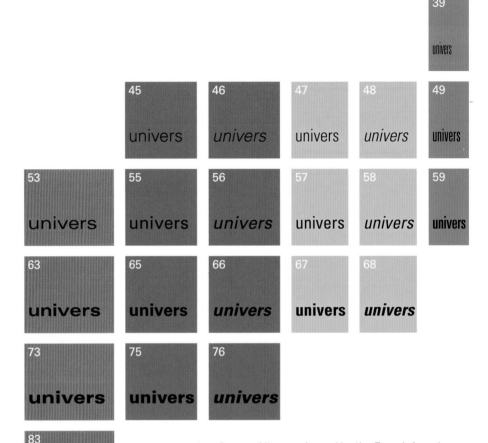

Right *The schematic originally designed by Adrian Frutiger to visually represent the complete Univers typeface family.*

No account of the International Typographic Style is complete without mentioning the two most famous typefaces to be designed during the 1950s. In 1954 Adrian Frutiger, a Swiss typeface designer based in Paris, completed design work on a new sans-serif named Univers that was arguably the world's first megafamily typeface as it comprised twenty-one individual weights. Frutiger expanded on the standard regular/italic/bold range to create a set of fonts each identified by a number—the family included expanded and condensed weights too. It took three years to produce all the weights as a commercially available typeface and it was released by the French foundry Deberny & Peignot in 1957, becoming enormously popular among Swiss-style typographers. In the mid-1950s, Eduard Hoffmann, the director of the HAAS Type Foundry in Münchenstein, Switzerland, decided that the ubiquitous Akzidenz Grotesk typeface was due an upgrade. In 1957 he worked with typeface designer Max Miedinger to create a new sans-serif typeface and named it Neue Haas Grotesk. A few years later, in 1960, the face was released by German foundry D. Stempel AG and was renamed Helvetica as a reference to the Latin name for Switzerland (*Confoederatio Helvetica*). The typeface went on to become the most popular sans-serif in the world and even got to star in its own self-titled movie by independent film maker Gary Hustwitt in 2007, celebrating the typeface's fiftieth birthday.

The International Typographic Style in America

It took until the late 1950s for the International Typographic Style to exert a firm grip on American graphic design. The business sector became interested in the style, seeing in it a more professional-looking and politically neutral style for the creation of corporate collateral. Existing style options that favored the use of illustration over photography were beginning to look out-of-date and, because the style displayed such a high level of neutrality, firms that wanted to appeal to the broadest stretch of people from the widest possible demographic range were keen to test its qualities. A survey of the best-known American corporate identities, many of which were designed during the late 1950s and the 1960s by the likes of Paul Rand (see pages 130–1) and Saul Bass (see pages 134–5), shows that the enduring appeal of the International Typographic Style worked very well in this particular application. Interestingly, it is largely the wholesale adoption of Swiss Style by corporate business which prompted the more liberal sections of 1960s society to seek alternative styles with which to express themselves visually.

Above *Classic logo designs by Paul Rand for United Parcel Service (UPS), designed in 1961, and Westinghouse, designed in 1960.*

 *is a trademark of Westinghouse Electric Corporation. All Rights Reserved*

New American advertising

In 1949 a new advertising agency named Doyle Dane Bernbach (DDB) opened for business at 350 Madison Avenue in New York City, and during the course of the 1950s it transformed the look of U.S. advertising. Using elements of the International Style and an approach which removed the boundaries between copy and image, it was fusing the two into one focussed concept where each element supported the other. At the same time, the agency introduced a new working method which would eventually become the accepted norm in agencies all over the world. Bill Bernbach understood that advertising on its own did not sell products; he realized that customers should be nurtured into a relationship with brands they were already minded to buy. He and his staff, originally consisting of art director Bob Gage and copywriter Phyllis Robinson, changed the traditional working method where a copywriter and an art director tended to work in isolation from each other, and instead worked in collaboration as a creative team. Every advertisement started with a concept rather than simply a "Buy This!"-style headline, and layouts would generally include only the elements entirely necessary to convey that concept, eschewing decoration and brash headline typography. The designs often included a single striking image which was not always a product shot; a cleanly set and concise headline that did not scream a stereotypical commercial message; and body copy that carried clear facts about the product without the inclusion of pointless superlatives. DDB art directors were not afraid to use white space, realizing that it could command as much, if not more, attention than cramped space, stuffed with as much information as possible.

One of their best-known campaigns was created for Volkswagen by art director Helmut Krone and copywriter Julian Koenig. The humorous approach of the "Think Small" campaign, with the original ad appearing in 1959, highlighted the simplicity of the car and was an eye-opener for the public. It has since been cited as the best print advertising campaign of the twentieth-century.

Left and opposite *The now famous Volkswagen advertisements created at Doyle Dane Bernbach by Helmut Krone and Julian Koenig set a new benchmark and inspired numerous art directors and copywriters to rethink the way products could be sold to the consumer. "Think Small" first appeared in 1959 with "Lemon", another addition to the campaign, following in 1960.*

Think small.

18 New York University students have gotten into a sun-roof VW; a tight fit. The Volkswagen is sensibly sized for a family. Mother, father, and three growing kids suit it nicely.

In economy runs, the VW averages close to 50 miles per gallon. You won't do near that; after all, professional drivers have canny trade secrets. (Want to know some? Write VW, Box #65, Englewood, N. J.) Use regular gas and forget about oil between changes.

The VW is 4 feet shorter than a conventional car (yet has as much leg room up front). While other cars are doomed to roam the crowded streets, you park in tiny places.

VW spare parts are inexpensive. A new front fender (at an *authorized* VW dealer) is $21.75.* A cylinder head, $19.95.* The nice thing is, they're seldom needed.

A new Volkswagen sedan is $1,565.* Other than a radio and side view mirror, that includes everything you'll really need.

 In 1959 about 120,000 Americans thought small and bought VWs. Think about it.

Paul Rand

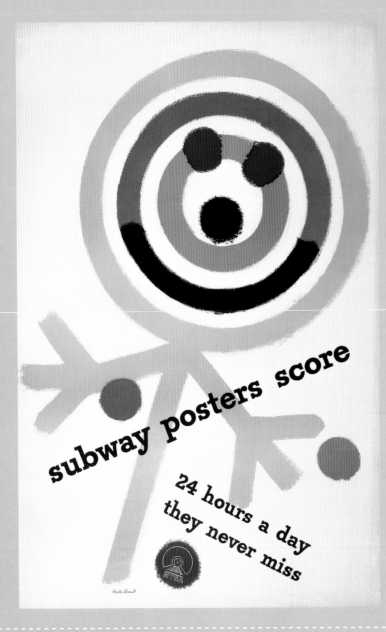

Below *An early Rand poster promoting advertising on the New York Subway, 1947.* **Collection Merrill C. Berman**

subway posters score

24 hours a day they never miss

Paul Rand was born Peretz Rosenbaum in New York in 1914 and received extensive design tuition at the Pratt Institute from 1929 to 1932, Parsons School of Design from 1932 to 1933, and the Art Students League from 1933 to 1934. Nonetheless, most of the visual vocabulary which influenced his later work came from the European books and magazines he collected— Rand mostly regarded himself as "self-taught." He is acclaimed as a key figure in the introduction of modernist styles to American graphic design and was a champion of the International Typographic Style.

Rand's career got off to an early and successful start with art-direction credits for *Esquire* and *Apparel* magazines in 1936 which rapidly earned him a full-time position, although he initially turned down the offer, for reasons of not being ready to take on the responsibility. Around this time he was also asked by editor Marguerite Tjader Harris to design covers for *Direction* magazine, which he shrewdly produced pro bono in return for a promise of full artistic freedom. This helped him to bolster his reputation amongst both his clients and his peers and to further develop his own personal style, a kind of European modernism with an American twist combining liberal doses of wit and metaphor. He was in fact reimbursed for his work at a later date with watercolor paintings by Le Corbusier.

Rand was one of the first American designers to commit his creative philosophy and visual approach to print, publishing his influential and highly regarded book *Thoughts on Design* in 1947. The book addressed the fundamental differences between the commercialism of American graphic design with the radical design styles originating from Europe. He felt strongly that the quality of creative input was often

EL PRODUCTO

every cigar says "merry christmas"

overlooked by clients in favor of simply creating pleasing layouts. The book is split into nine sections covering subjects such as "The Symbol in Advertising," "The Role of Humor," and "Typographic Form and Expression," all illustrated with Rand's own work.

Despite this significant body of work, Rand's enduring links to graphic design are via his numerous corporate identity projects for many high-profile companies that are still in use today, including Westinghouse, UPS (United Parcel Service, albeit in a revised form), and of course IBM (International Business Machines). His first logo for IBM was drawn in 1956 and acquired its distinctive stripes in 1972. His logos were typically minimal and unfussy—as Rand himself put it, a logo "cannot survive unless it is designed with the utmost simplicity and restraint."

Rand continued to work through the 1980s and 1990s, appearing on one of the famous "Think Different" posters produced by Apple. He died in 1996, shortly after Apple cofounder and chairman Steve Jobs had referred to him as "the greatest living graphic designer."

Top *Rand enjoyed a long working relationship with the El Producto cigar company and designed many advertisements for them during the 1940s and 1950s.* **Collection Merrill C. Berman**

Above *The two variations of Rand's famous logo for IBM (International Business Machines). The original solid version was designed in 1956 and remained in use until the stripes were added in 1972.*

Cipe Pineles

Her first job was for the collective Contempora Ltd., experimenting with textile designs which, in turn, piqued her interest in women's fashion, and her work caught the eye of magazine publisher Condé Nast who offered her a position in the design department in 1932, working under art director Mehemed Fehmy Agha.

Agha had transformed *Vogue's* old-fashioned look since his arrival at the company, using modernist styles such as Art Deco and Constructivism (see pages 70–1, 62–5) and introducing the use of white space and full-bleed images. Illustration, previously a mainstay of magazines like *Vogue*, gave way to photography, and typography was brought up to date through the use of new sans-serif typefaces such as Futura. He encouraged Pineles to apply his experimental approach to her layouts for *Vogue* and *Vanity Fair*, and she took to the challenge with relish, building her skills as an art director and editorial designer along the way. This led to her appointment in 1942 as the art director for *Glamour*, the first time a woman had held such a senior position in magazine publishing.

In turn, and after a brief period working in Paris on a magazine for servicewomen during World War Two, Pineles moved on to become art director of *Seventeen* magazine, one of the earliest publications of its kind aimed specifically at a teenage market. *Seventeen* was different from other magazines from that period as it treated its readership more seriously, with unpatronizing articles and feature articles geared toward intelligent young adults rather than giggling children. This provided the opportunity for Pineles to commission some of the best photographers and

Rightly or wrongly, Cipe Pineles is remembered in the history of twentieth century graphic design for being an important female figure in what was a male-driven industry. She was the first woman to become the art director of a mainstream American magazine, and the first woman to become a member of the New York Art Directors Club which was previously an all-male institution. Gender identification aside, she was one of the finest art directors working in the U.S. from the 1930s to the early 1960s. Born in 1908 in Vienna, Austria, Pineles emigrated to America with her family in 1923 and studied graphic design at the Pratt Institute in New York from 1926 to 1929.

artists of the day to illustrate the spreads, and her reputation grew further with the supportive patronage of editor and founder Helen Valentine. Pineles stayed at *Seventeen* for three years before moving on to art-direct *Charm* magazine in 1950, and finally the magazine *Mademoiselle* in 1960.

By 1961 Pineles had become a freelance consultant and discovered a passion for design education which led to her taking up a position teaching editorial design at Parsons School of Design, something she continued to do until the mid-1980s before finally deciding to retire. While with the school she also conducted the promotional program with students, providing design and photographic services. Pineles died in 1991.

Opposite *Pineles became art director of* Seventeen *magazine in 1947 after returning to the U.S. from Paris. The cover shown is the July 1949 edition.*

Left Charm *was a fashion magazine aimed at women working between leaving school and getting married (attitudes to women's roles were of course quite different in the 1950s). Pineles art-directed the magazine for ten years between 1950 and 1960—this striking cover is the January 1954 issue.*

Saul Bass

Over the years, Saul Bass's work has arguably been viewed by more people than any other graphic designer's. Known for his numerous successful corporate identity projects, he was also the undisputed master of the movie title sequence, creating memorable designs for films such as *The Man With the Golden Arm*, *Vertigo*, *North by North West*, *Psycho*, and *West Side Story* to name but a few. In the new era of DVDs and on-demand movie watching, even those viewers eager to skip to the beginning of the action tend not to watch Saul Bass's title sequences on fast-forward.

Born in New York in 1920, Bass took evening classes at the Art Students League in Manhattan in 1936 before landing his first proper graphic design position for a small advertising firm about a year later. Several further moves found him working for the Blaine Thompson Company, a well-regarded New York advertising agency, and it was during this time that he met the Bauhaus luminary György Kepes. Kepes was teaching at Brooklyn College and, as an admirer of Kepes's writings and reputation, Bass immediately enrolled on his course. It was here that Bass learned about the Modern Movement in graphic design, and Kepes's interest in the links between graphic design and movies arguably informed much of the direction that Bass's career subsequently took.

Bass was offered a position working in 1946 for Buchanan and Company who ran accounts for big clients such as TWA (Trans World Airlines) and Paramount Pictures, and he leapt at the opportunity, relocating to Los Angeles. By 1952, Bass had decided to open his own office and in 1956, he hired Elaine Makatura as a design assistant. They married in 1961 and collaborated on projects for the rest of Bass's life.

Bass is one of the best examples of a mid-century modern designer that somehow had the ability to turn his hand to just about anything including graphic design, product and packaging design, film (of course), and even architecture. His title sequences and posters for films directed by the likes of Otto Preminger, Alfred Hitchcock, and in later years Martin Scorsese are legendary and were always groundbreaking. Though not his most famous, his sequence for *Grand Prix* (1966) is particularly interesting as it uses multiple close shots of race cars sharply edited in order to build to the start of the Monte Carlo Grand Prix, leading seamlessly into the narrative of the movie. He directed all the footage used for the sequence and director John Frankenheimer was so impressed he asked Bass to act as overall visual consultant for the film—Bass shot the footage for all but one of the races shown. He had also been involved in storyboarding and shooting the famous shower scene in *Psycho* for Hitchcock in 1960, and in 1968 won an Oscar for his short documentary *Why Man Creates*.

In contrast to his film work, Bass designed many prominent and enduring logos for a number of important companies including Continental Airlines (1968), Rockwell International (1968), Bell Telephone (1969), Quaker Oats (1969), United Airlines (1974), Warner Communications (1974), Minolta (1978), Geffen Records (1980), AT&T Globe (1983), and NCR Corporation (1996). Those of his logos that have since gone out of use have done so mainly because companies have either folded or merged, and the average lifespan of a Bass logo has been calculated to be 34 years. Bass died in Los Angeles in 1996.

Above *One of Bass' best known movie posters designed to promote Alfred Hitchcock's* Vertigo, *1961.*

Below *Logo for Continental Airlines, 1967.*

Neue H

Optima

Courier

Mistral

Helvet

aas

Choc

Palatino

Univers

Melior

ca ✳

The early 1950s witnessed the start of the economic recovery following World War Two and the design industry gradually moved back on track. The demand for innovative new print solutions, particularly in the area of advertising, increased rapidly throughout the decade and early inroads into photosetting—over hot metal, typesetting's previously unchallenged dominance—provided fresh opportunities for type designers to create new faces to fuel the burgeoning market.

Palatino
Hermann Zapf | 1950

Banco
Roger Excoffon | 1951

Melior
Hermann Zapf | 1952

Mistral
Roger Excoffon | 1953

Choc
Roger Excoffon | 1954

Courier
Howard Kettler | 1955

Neue Haas
Max Miedinger, Eduard Hoffmann | 1957

Helvetica
*Max Miedinger, Eduard Hoffmann,
Arthur Ritzel (responsible for the expansion
of the Helvetica family for Stempel) | 1957–60*

Univers
Adrian Frutiger | 1957

Optima
Hermann Zapf | 1958

Melior

ABCDEFGHIJKLM
NOPQRSTUVWXYZ
abcdefghijklm
nopqrstuvwxyz
1234567890
(.,:;?!$£&-*){ÀÓÜÇ}

Melior, designed by Hermann Zapf in 1952 for Linotype, is one of the few serif typefaces with round letterforms based on a shape known as a superellipse. A superellipse is an oval which has sides that are almost flat, and the shape is more often utilized in the design of sans-serif typefaces. Zapf intended the typeface to be suitable for use in narrow newspaper columns and short passages of text, and its clear readability fulfills this goal very well. It would be true to say that Melior is a typeface of its time and does look slightly dated if used in a twenty-first-century context, but it is a perfect choice for text that needs to conjure up a 1950s or 1960s vibe.

Choc

ABCDEFGHIJKLM
NOPQRSTUVWXYZ
abcdefghijklm
nopqrstuvwxyz
1234567890
(.,:;?!$£&-*){ÀÓÜÇ}

The 1950s witnessed a resurgence in interest in typefaces that mimicked handwritten typographic forms, with a particular focus on those designed for use by the advertising industry. Perhaps the most notable purveyor of typefaces of this kind during the period was the French designer Roger Excoffon and the Marseille-based company Fonderie Olive. Excoffon designed five typefaces with a distinct hand-lettered flavor during the 1950s; Banco, Mistral, Diane, Calypso, and in 1954 Choc; all of which were published by Fonderie Olive. With the exception of Diane, which was drawn as a formal script, all were designed primarily for the French advertising industry and garnered a large following, providing a distinctively Gallic character to much of the graphic design produced during the decade.

Helvetica

ABCDEFGHIJKLM
NOPQRSTUVWXYZ
abcdefghijklm
nopqrstuvwxyz
1234567890
(.,:;?!$£&-*){ÀÓÜÇ}

Helvetica, which we also discuss on page 126, is the sans-serif typeface that everyone has heard of but it began life with a different name. Until 1960 it was known as Neue Haas Grotesk but was rechristened Helvetica during commercial production at D. Stempel AG—the name is derived from *Helvetia*, the Latin name for Switzerland. It was designed in 1957 by Max Miedinger and Eduard Hoffmann as a modern equivalent to the aged Akzidenz Grotesk and was used religiously by designers working in the Swiss Style during the 1960s and 1970s. Today most professional designers use Neue Helvetica (shown here), a 1983 revision designed at D. Stempel AG and released by Linotype, which unifies the various styles designed over the years into a numerical classification similar to that employed by Univers.

Optima

ABCDEFGHIJKLM
NOPQRSTUVWXYZ
abcdefghijklm
nopqrstuvwxyz
1234567890
(.,:;?!$£&-*){ÀÓÜÇ}

The prolific typeface designer Hermann Zapf began working on the drawings for Optima in 1952 but the design world had to wait until 1958 for D. Stempel AG to release it. A humanist sans-serif typeface, Optima (like other typefaces from the same classification) was designed to counter the argument that sans-serifs were characterless and difficult to read. The variable-width strokes and calligraphic aesthetics of Optima give us a warmer typeface with a touch of the handmade that feels a little like a sans-serif and a little like a serif at the same time. It is flexible enough to work as both a text and a display font, which is no mean feat, and although it can look somewhat dated when used out of context it remains a popular choice among designers.

The Council of Industrial Design

August 1958   No 116   Price 3s

Design

GARLAND

The traditional **slab-serif** style typeface of the masthead was set to be replaced by a more contemporary **sans-serif** by 1962.

The inclusion of the aircraft motif acts almost like an identity for the issue. The use of icons and graphic symbolism enjoyed a surge in popularity throughout the 1940s and 1950s alongside the emergence of the **International Typographic Style**.

The use of an image depicting figures climbing a staircase in combination with the arrow motifs is a cleverly conceived visual trick which strongly suggests upward movement, an important aspect of the airplane activity at any airport.

Despite the type being heavily cropped at each side, the distinctive name of London 's second airport at Gatwick is immediately evident to any British readers.

Design magazine

Ken Garland | 1958

Design magazine was launched in the United Kingdom in 1949 as a mouthpiece for the Council of Industrial Design, the body that would later become the Design Council in 1972. British designer Ken Garland took on the art direction of the magazine in 1955, just one year after graduating from London's Central School of Arts and Crafts, and immediately brought a visual freshness which helped raise the awareness of contemporary graphic design within the area of British industrial design.

Garland commissioned the first few covers during his tenure—they were created by noted graphic designer F. H. K. Henrion—but soon began to design the covers and interiors himself and injected a combination of visual flair, bold statement, and humor which completely transformed the look of the publication. Many cover designs included stylized or abstract elements used to illustrate the principal features within each issue. The example shown here, which coincided with a new phase of development at Gatwick, London's second international airport, features arrow motifs and figures climbing a staircase, conjuring the sense of an upward trajectory.

The color palette row below is a sampler of colors selected from the *Design* magazine cover shown here and is representative of the range of colors a designer working in this style might have used during the 1950s.

c =	000%	000%	000%	040%	045%	080%	070%	000%
m =	000%	085%	090%	055%	090%	050%	080%	000%
y =	070%	060%	025%	055%	030%	040%	050%	000%
k =	000%	000%	000%	050%	020%	030%	070%	100%

1960s

Ask any historian which decade of the 20th century they feel was the most important in terms of the progress of social development, and the likely response will be "the 60s." The younger generation had had enough of aping their parents, lifestyles and aspirations, they were ready to break free of the conservatism of their peers, and graphic design was destined to play a big part in bringing their message to the world.

The end of World War Two marked the beginning of a population surge throughout the U.S. and western Europe, the "baby boom" as it is known today, when an estimated seventy-six million children were born in America alone between 1945 and 1964. By the early 1960s, the original baby boomers had grown into teenagers with a newly acquired lust for life and a desire to make things different. The global economy did not exist in the form it does today of course, but the postwar economic boom enjoyed by the U.S. gradually radiated outwards, particularly in the direction of its European trading partners. By the beginning of the 60s the rather severe, pared-back design sensibilities that people had grown used to as a part of their everyday lives were on their way out —things were about to become a whole lot brighter. This new society of young, educated, and politically aware people were to become the driving force behind the greatest cultural upheaval for generations, and a previously unseen explosion of design creativity rode in on that wave of nonconformist change.

The youth subculture of the 1960s—if you like, a less introspective version of the Beat Generation of the 1950s—fully embraced graphic design as a way to spread their message on a global scale, and the predominant styles that emerged throughout the decade grew to reflect the hedonistic values which underpinned the cultural upheaval. It would be inaccurate to state that the 1960s marked the end of Modernism, as elements of the style continued to feature prominently (as Mid-Century Modern and Late Modern) in work created throughout the decade. Elements of Modernism in its various forms are to this day still strongly evident in contemporary graphic design, but the decade provides a marker for the point at which the discipline of Modernism's form and function began to make room for a greater stylistic freedom in graphic design and typography. By the beginning of the decade the original socially progressive ideals of Modernist graphic design had to a certain extent been hijacked by the corporate world—alternative design styles which reflected the more liberal and open-minded attitudes of 1960s society were needed.

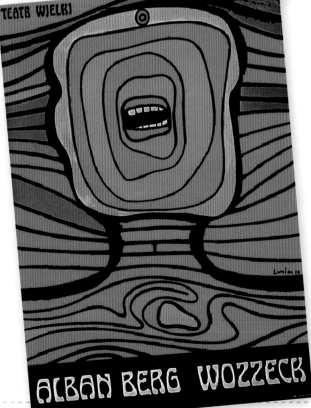

Above *From the early 1960s Rudolph de Harak designed almost 400 covers for publisher McGraw-Hill Paperbacks. Influenced by a combination of movements including Abstract Expressionism and Op art, each cover featured Akzidenz Grotesk as the principal typeface, plus a single photograph or illustration which communicated the book's content in a purely visual way.*

Left *A Jan Lenica poster for the 1964 production of Wozzeck by the Warsaw Opera. Lenica's angsty, expressionist style had developed over a period of some 15 years, and he was an influential founder of the highly regarded Polish School of Posters.*

Pop Art

Pop Art's origins lie in two different strands, emerging first in Britain in the mid-1950s and in the U.S. in the later part of the decade. This vibrant art movement and its subsequent influences on graphic design set out to challenge fine art traditions—particularly Abstract Expressionism which was still very much in vogue as one of the true postwar American art movements—through its direct reference to and utilization of elements from popular culture; advertising, newspapers, magazines, and comic books. By the early 1960s this combination of fine art and graphics began to strongly influence commercial graphic design and manifested itself in all areas of mainstream visual culture, especially music and fashion graphics.

Arguably, Pop Art was based wholly on American cultural references, but the British and U.S. styles were noticeably different in character. In Britain the general idea of visual irony and off-the-wall parody which underpins the Pop Art style were certainly in evidence but, in addition, much of the graphic design produced during this period perceptibly acknowledged the notion of the newly realized prosperity and associated affluence emerging from the States. The references to the increasing influence of American popular culture on the everyday lives of people in Britain and the rest of western Europe were ever present. Also, an element of nostalgia less evident in American Pop Art graphics of the time helped define and therefore set apart British Pop Art. By contrast, and bearing in mind that American designers were already fully immersed in the cultural influences emanating from their own country, the U.S. Pop Art style was more about the satire to be found in the representation of everyday objects as art—think Andy Warhol's soup cans, for example—and about the diffusion of the more painterly disciplines of the abstract expressionists. In that sense, one can draw direct parallels between Pop Art and what the Dadaists were doing with collage 40 years earlier, but with less social anarchy and more sarcasm in the case of Pop Art.

Early pieces of work such as the collage *I was a Rich Man's Plaything* created by the Scottish artist and sculptor Eduardo Paolozzi in 1947, and Richard Hamilton's *Just what is it that makes today's homes so different, so appealing?*, dated 1956, are considered precursors of the Pop Art movement. Hamilton also provides an interesting insight into the early perceptions of Pop Art. In a 1957 letter to British architects Alison and Peter Smithson, he states its qualities as "popular, transient, low cost, mass produced, young, witty, sexy, gimmicky, glamorous, big business." The final entry of this list says a lot about how the commercial opportunities of this "mass appeal" visual style resonated with both artists and graphic designers. However, despite its earlier beginnings, it was not until the 1960s that the style began to achieve mainstream impetus and exert its influence on graphic designers. In Britain, Pop Art provided the visual personification of "The Swinging Sixties" with flamboyant typography and colorfully bold graphics emblazoned across record covers, T-shirts, and the store fronts of London's Carnaby Street and King's Road. British Pop artist Peter Blake cocreated the cover for *Sgt. Pepper's Lonely Hearts Club Band* with his then wife Jann Haworth in 1967, while in the same year Andy Warhol created the peeling banana sleeve for the Velvet Underground album that carried his name. Warhol—who initially trained as a commercial illustrator—famously declared that vernacular "popular" culture was a legitimate basis for fine art and successfully combined art and graphics to create a complete lifestyle. In doing so he helped provide the inspiration for designers to reference a broader range of influences, thus bringing Postmodernism another step closer.

SHOW

THE MAGAZINE OF THE ARTS

75 CENTS
APRIL 1963

INCORPORATING USA · 1

TOO MANY KENNEDYS? by ALISTAIR COOKE

Opposite *Designed by Andy Warhol himself in 1967, the* Velvet Underground's *debut album featured a peelable banana sticker and the instruction "Peel slowly and see." Reissued vinyl editions of the album do not include the sticker, making the originals highly collectible.*

Left Show *was a monthly U.S. arts magazine that ran from 1961 to 1964. Art director Henry Wolf, backed by designer Sam Antupit, demonstrated a brilliant knack for creating covers that referenced the work of painters and graphic artists, such as the April 1963 Warhol-influenced edition—the U.S. flag is made from portraits of JFK, his wife Jackie, and daughter Caroline.*

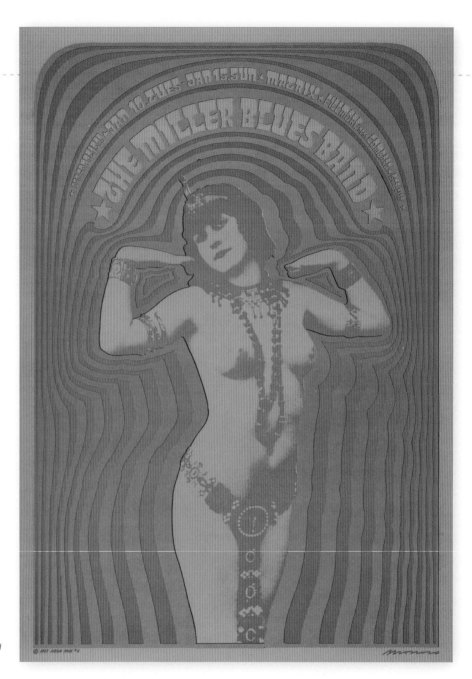

Right *This 1967 poster by Victor Moscoso is a fine example of the psychedelic style, combining Pop Art and Victoriana to great effect.*

Psychedelia

The word "psychedelic" was first coined by British psychologist Humphry Osmond in 1957 following his research into hallucinogenic substances and in turn was adopted to describe the style of psychedelic art. The open-minded liberalism mentioned earlier in this chapter was certainly due in part to a sharp increase in the use of hallucinogenic drugs such as LSD during the 1960s by groups of young malcontents unhappy with the way society still insisted on indoctrinating younger generations in the moralistic values which they deemed outdated. American psychologist Timothy Leary encouraged American youth to "turn on, tune in, and drop out" and thousands of young people flocked to the mecca of hippiedom, the U.S. west coast and in particular San Francisco, to do just that.

Psychedelia is very much a style that emerged out of a social context—it answered the need for a rejoinder to the increasingly corporate feel of the International Style that had dominated during the previous decade. Drawing on the historical influences of Victoriana, Art Nouveau, Dada, and of course the relatively current Pop Art movement, a loosely formed group of, for the most part, untrained young designers living in the San Francisco Bay area developed an expressionistic visual style that became Psychedelic Design. Notable among these were Rick Griffin, Alton Kelley, Victor Moscoso, Stanley Miller (better known as Stanley Mouse), and Wes Wilson (profiled on page 152–3); now collectively referred to as the "Big Five" of Psychedelia. Much of their work took the form of

posters commissioned by music promoters working in the flourishing Californian scene, with some of the finest examples being those which advertised rock concerts promoted by Bill Graham at the Fillmore Auditorium. Possibly due to the general lack of formal graphic design schooling among the main protagonists of the movement, and certainly to refute the principal components of modernist illustration and typography, Psychedelic Design placed little emphasis on legibility, preferring instead to give free reign to the underlying expressionist principles of the style. Graham would sometimes insist on additional notes set in more legible typefaces in the margins of posters to ensure that potential concert goers could check that they had read the information correctly. Throughout its heyday Psychedelic Design continued to combine a heady mix of borrowed historical styles without concerning itself with the baggage of the political or moral ideologies that accompanied them, so in that regard Psychedelia represents perfectly the sense of freedom that indelibly associates itself with the 1960s.

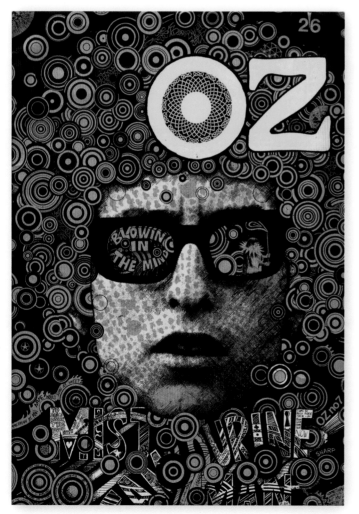

Left *This October 1967 cover of Oz magazine was based entirely on an earlier Bob Dylan poster by designer Martin Sharp which drew heavily on the influence of psychedelic art.*

1960s

Op Art and the Olympics

Op Art, or Optical Art as it also known, draws influences collectively from Cubism, Futurism, Constructivism, and Dada, but is arguably more precisely related to the constructivist teachings of the Bauhaus (see page 68–70). The phrase "Op Art" first appeared in a *Time* magazine article in October 1964 covering the New York show of Julian Stanczak's "Optical Paintings" which used bold lines and contrasting colors to create the optical illusion that the images were actually vibrating on the canvas. This was not the first time that work of this kind had been produced, but many artists, Stanczak included, had shunned the term, preferring the term "perceptual" art.

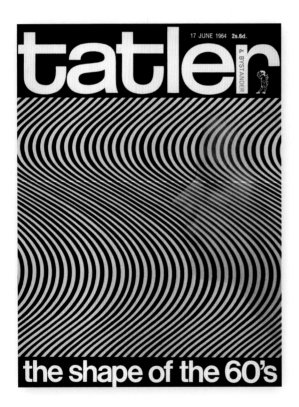

Above *The cover of British fashion and lifestyle magazine* Tatler *from June 17, 1964 featured a piece created by the well known Op Art artist Bridget Riley.*

As an art movement, Op art was not a massive hit with many critics who tended to regard the work as simply optical illusion or *trompe-l'oeil* with little beyond a novelty appeal. However, the general public loved it and this did not go unnoticed by graphic designers who, where appropriate, began to use Op Art techniques to accomplish their own commercial projects. Op Art imagery began to show up everywhere from print and television advertising to album cover art and home furnishings. Fabric design was particularly well suited to the Op Art treatment and the fashion industry took full advantage of the trend, producing clothing and accessories emblazoned with eye-challenging Op Art designs.

Among the many graphic design projects produced during the 1960s which reference the style, there is one that has become a genuine design classic. For many years graphic designers the world over had been promoting the idea that comprehensive signage and branding systems were vital for large international public events, and the 60s marked a turning point where graphic designers and planners came together to turn the concept into a reality. The 19th Olympic Games held in Mexico City in 1968 provided American designer Lance Wyman, alongside British industrial designer Peter Murdoch, with probably the finest opportunity up to that point to create a complete information system of signage, pictograms (which were immune to issues of language), and publicity. The end result of two years of work is rightly regarded as one of the most successful design systems ever created, but the standout of the whole project is the stunning logo which combines elements of Aztec and Mexican folk art with an Op Art-style execution composed of repeated parallel rules flowing outward from the type. The logo was developed further into a display typeface which was subsequently used on everything from tickets and clothing to billboards, and helped provide Op Art with its place in graphic design history.

Although the Op Art trend really only lasted for a few years, as an official movement its appeal has endured. Indeed, the manual skills required to create Op Art style visuals in the 60s have been largely supplanted by computer software capable of calculating the precise dimensions and spacing for each stripe or circle. However, try designing with a brush or a pen and you will soon realize that it is not as easy as some of its critics would have you think.

Above and left *Lance Wyman's famous Mexico 68 Olympic logo.* **Sketch: Lance Wyman; Poster: Lance Wyman (design), Eduardo Terrazas and Pedro Ramirez Vasquez (art direction); Photograph: Lance Wyman.**

The advent of "in-house" typesetting

Until the late 1950s, typesetting was limited to the constraints of "hot metal" type composed on Linotype and Monotype machines. Installation of these large, heavy machines was pretty much impossible outside of print shops and dedicated typesetting firms with the space and facilities to operate them. However, during the 1950s and 1960s the development of a new

Above *French typographer Robert Massin created this groundbreaking book as an interpretation of Eugène Ionesco's play* La Cantatrice Chauve *in 1964. Each character is assigned their own separate typeface and female characters always "speak" in italics. Without phototypesetting and the ongoing switch from letterpress to lithographic printing the book would have been practically impossible to produce in this form.*

typesetting process took place and the rolling out of the "cold type" or phototypesetting system by a number of competing companies marked a major event in typographic history. The earliest phototypesetting machines simply projected individual characters onto film—characters were then transferred to paper using an offset printing process — and the quality of the setting was not always good when compared to hot metal. Furthermore, graphic designers with no prior compositing experience were suddenly provided with an opportunity to set their own type, but without the skills acquired over many years by typesetting professionals the results were not always successful. Poor letter spacing, ugly word and line breaks, and distorted letter forms abounded—a situation which would interestingly repeat itself some years later with the advent of PostScript and desktop publishing. However, rapid developments in computer technology allowed typesetting to be previewed on a CRT (cathode ray tube) screen-using software to control letter spacing and line-breaks. This did not necessarily solve the lack-of-skills issue on the part of the operator as the programs were far from perfect, but lowered costs and increased convenience meant that phototypesetting gradually replaced hot metal as the first choice for many graphic designers. Some purists stuck with hot metal for as long as possible and, because of the large initial investment in printing plant, the newspaper industry was the last to lose hot metal as its main method for typesetting. By the 1980s hot metal setting could only be commercially sourced from specialist firms.

Another significant development which helped bring typesetting in-house for graphic designers was the launch of dry-transfer lettering by Letraset in 1961. Practically everyone of a certain age, whether a designer or not, will remember the plastic sheets containing a selection of characters from a particular typeface which could be transferred to more or less any smooth surface by rubbing over each character using a flat-ended stylus (or the end of a biro if that was all you had to hand). Letraset was somewhat limited in that it was only really suitable for headline setting, although smaller point sizes were available, but the rub-down technique was easy to master and was a relatively low-cost option for design studios.

As well as maintaining its own type design program, Letraset also licensed typefaces from existing foundries and created their products using the original drawings, meaning Letraset headline setting was often more faithful to the original typeface design than photosetting. Once again, serious visual crimes were often committed by those who lacked the honed typesetting skills of a seasoned professional, but the huge selection of typefaces that grew along with Letraset's popularity provided many more creative options for designers than were previously available. Remarkably you can still purchase Letraset, although there are only a handful of typefaces now available.

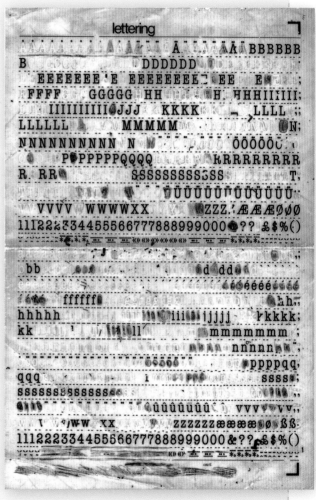

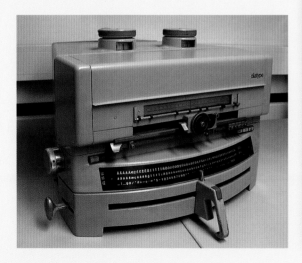

Above *Berthold's Diatype machine was designed to set headlines rather than running text. Each character of a given typeface could be selected from a glass master plate using the trigger mechanism, then exposed onto film for printing and paste-up.*

Above *A partially used sheet of Letraset demonstrating how a variety of implements were often used to transfer each letter to the artwork.*

Wes Wilson

BILL GRAHAM PRESENTS IN SAN FRANCISCO

Above *An example of Wilson's work for Bill Graham and the Fillmore, this 1967 poster advertises concerts on consecutive nights by Otis Rush Chicago Blues Band, Grateful Dead and the Canned Heat Blues Band.*

There is no better example of a graphic style born out of social context than that of the psychedelic rock posters that began to appear in California in 1965, and one of the finest proponents of the style was Robert Wesley "Wes" Wilson, born in Sacramento, California in 1937. Like many of his fellow designers of the time, Wilson had no formal training; he actually studied forestry and horticulture before dropping out of college in 1963. He moved to the Bay Area of San Francisco in 1965 and began to self-publish work, his first pieces being posters protesting against the war in Vietnam.

A meeting and subsequent business partnership with a printer, Bob Carr, led to Wilson's increased involvement in the Beat poetry and jazz scene. This led to further work for a number of music promoters—most significantly for Bill Graham and the Fillmore Auditorium— which produced many of Wilson's best-known pieces. His work profoundly reflects the attitude of counterculture and the burgeoning drug scene adopted by many young people during this period, and the acknowledged influence of Art Nouveau references the idealism of an earlier, equally edgy time. If one compares his well-known 1966 lithographic poster promoting a Captain Beefheart concert at the Fillmore with Alfred Roller's 1903 poster for the Vienna Secession 16 exhibition (see page 30) the similarity of the space-filling lettering style immediately leaps out. Typographic legibility is sacrificed in favor of visual form, which in the case of this poster is somewhat fortunate as "Beefheart" has been misspelled as "Beefhart," but one doubts that

TICKETS **SAN FRANCISCO:** City Lights Bookstore; The Psychedelic Shop; Mnasidika; Bally Lo (Union Square); The Town Squire (1318 Polk); S. F. State College; **BERKELEY:** Campus Records; Discount Records; Shakespeare & Co.; **MILL VALLEY:** Valerie Ann's; **SAUSALITO:** The Tides Bookstore; **MENLO PARK:** Kepler's Bookstore.

Left *Perhaps more than any other of Wilson's posters, the 1966 artwork promoting a Captain Beefhart (sic) concert at The Fillmore Auditorium demonstrates the stylistic links between Art Nouveau and Psychedelia.*

anyone was overly concerned about this at the time. Having said that, Bill Graham would sometimes repeat information using a regular typeface in the margins of the poster to ensure viewers could double-check dates and ticket outlets.

This comparison with the Viennese Secessionists is by no means unfavorable, as referencing earlier historical design styles is generally a key aspect of Postmodernism, and Wilson often mixed Art Nouveau lettering and illustration style with found images

drawn from Victorian ephemera. It was the combination of these different historical styles and the fact that many of the contemporary viewers would have no direct knowledge of Wilson's influences that made the style look so fresh at the time. At the time of writing, Wilson still paints and designs the occasional poster for projects that capture his interest.

Push Pin Studios

Push Pin Studio began life as a collaboration between four graduates of the Cooper Union art school in New York: Seymour Chwast (born in Bronx, New York, in 1931), Reynold Ruffins (born in New York City in 1930), Edward Sorel (born in Bronx, New York, in 1929), and Milton Glaser (born in New York City in 1929). First formed in 1954 after Chwast and Sorel left their jobs at *Esquire* magazine on the same day and by using their unemployment checks to rent a flat in Manhattan as studio space, Glaser joined Push Pin a few months later on completion of a year's study in Bologna, Italy. By 1958 Chwast and Glaser were the sole partners.

From its formation onwards, the firm had set out to establish an eclectic style of its own which did not follow the principles of Modernism and the International Style. Glaser had studied etching under the Italian artist Giorgio Morandi and was particularly interested in the Italian Renaissance style of painting, whilst Chwast was absorbed by the qualities of nineteenth century wood type as used in historical American print advertising. Other shared sources of inspiration ranging from Victorian ephemera, Art Nouveau, and Art Deco to vernacular comic and cartoon art meant the pair were well placed to help initiate a move away from the accepted modernist typographic style and the rigid imposition of the grid. Though it would be inaccurate to state that they fully rejected the basic principles which govern modern functional graphic design, Push Pin was certainly instrumental in championing decoration as an acceptable component of mainstream graphic design. One could almost describe

Chwast and Glaser as revivalists in the sense that for the first time in thirty or so years they made it OK to once again reference and combine styles from earlier historical periods in order to create something fresh.

Their main contribution to the graphic design industry is arguably the reestablishment of illustration as a popular option for designers in the face of a progressively dominant requirement for the realism provided by photography. During the 1950s, art directors increasingly chose photography as an illustrative medium, often under pressure from clients

Opposite *Seymour Chwast's 1968 poster* Judy Garland *is a typical example of the way the studio favored illustration over photography. Many of the fresh illustrative styles developed at Push Pin went on to influence generations of graphic designers and illustrators.*

Left *Milton Glaser's iconic 1966* Dylan *poster sold over six million copies. He based the silhouetted outline of Dylan's face on a Marcel Duchamp self-portrait and later remarked how ironic it was that the poster was subsequently deemed a quintessentially American graphic design style.*

who wanted to present their products exactly as they appeared in real life. The alternative offered by Push Pin allowed wit and visual interpretation back into the mix, given that the natural boundaries presented by photography, at the time at least, were irrelevant for talented designers or illustrators. This combination of visual eclecticism and hand-drawn aesthetic puts Push Pin Studio firmly in pole position as one of the main forerunners of the Postmodern design style.

The partnership ended in 1974 when Glaser left to establish Milton Glaser Inc., but Chwast continues to maintain the Push Pin name to the present day.

Herb Lubalin

Herb Lubalin, born in New York in 1918, is regarded as one of the most notable art directors of the mid-twentieth century, particularly for his innovative contributions to magazine design and layout, and for his groundbreaking typography and type design. As with many of his contemporaries, the cultural climate of the 1960s encouraged him to broadly spurn Modernist principles and the International Style in favor of a more open approach to his work which drew on a considerably greater set of eclectic inspirations.

Lubalin graduated from the Cooper Union art school, New York, in 1939 and initially found it difficult to secure regular work, but eventually landed the job of art director at healthcare communications specialist Sudler & Hennessey (now part of Young & Rubicam), enabling him to hone his already broadening skill set and to commission and collaborate with some of the best creatives

working in the U.S. at that time, including fashion and music photographer Art Kane, art director George Lois, and designer/illustrator Seymour Chwast. After almost 20 years with Sudler & Hennessey, Lubalin left in 1964 to form his own design firm, Herb Lubalin Inc.

Much of Lubalin's work opts to reject the relative constraints of functionalism in favor of a more expressive style of typography which blurs the lines between text and image. Some of his best-known pieces are really typographic illustrations which articulate their meaning visually as well as through the choice of wording. Significantly, the introduction of phototypesetting (see page 150) enabled him to experiment with type in ways that had been inaccessible with hot-metal type—characters could be distorted (in a good way in Lubalin's case) and combined to form dynamic headlines and display type, and the increased range of available point sizes allowed him to push the boundaries of magazine layout to new levels.

Lubalin art-directed three important magazines during the 1960s; *Eros* (four issues between 1962 and 1963); *Fact* (22 issues between 1965 and 1967); and *Avant Garde* (14 issues between 1968 and 1971). All were published by Ralph Ginzburg, an author and photojournalist best known for publishing books and magazines on art and erotica. *Eros* was dedicated to documenting 1960s counterculture and the burgeoning rise of sexual liberation, was produced using different paper stocks in a large format, and, unusually, carried no advertising. Unfortunately, the magazine ceased publication following an obscenity trial brought by the U.S. Postal Service. *Fact*, partly as a response to the authorities' attitude to *Eros* magazine, carried editorial written by writers who would normally find it difficult to publish their work in mainstream media and was firmly antiestablishment. Unlike the elegant design approach of *Eros*, *Fact* was designed minimally and printed in black and white on uncoated paper stock, allowing the boldness of the content to speak for itself. Legal action by the

Republican presidential candidate Barry Goldwater eventually forced the magazine to close. *Avant Garde* marked a return to higher production values and, once again, featured risqué (for the time at least) content including nudity, strong language, and criticism of American society and the Government. It was the most successful magazine of the three, drawing its large audience from readers involved in the New York design scene. When Ginzburg was eventually imprisoned in 1972 as a result of the ongoing legal issues surrounding the *Eros* trial, publication of *Avant Garde* had already ceased in 1971. The magazine's logotype eventually went on to become a complete typeface, ITC Avant Garde Gothic, issued through the International Typeface Corporation which Lubalin cofounded with Aaron Burns and Edward Rondthaler in 1970. His magazine work and innovative typographic pieces remain as fresh today as they were thirty or more years ago, indicating just how contemporary Lubalin's ideas were. Lubalin died in New York in 1981.

Opposite *Eros ran for only four issues but the design of the magazine and the highly charged yet non-gratuitous content made it one of the most admired publications of its day.*

Above left Fact, *the follow-up to Eros, was overtly antiestablishment and covers often carried controversial social or political statements.*

Left and below *Another controversial publication,* Avant Garde *ran for 16 issues and produced its own typeface, based on the logo and drawn by Lubalin and Tom Carnase. The covers featured a single striking illustration and, unusually, just the logo with no additional tag lines.*

Hawthorn

Antique

Snell Rou

Syntax

Amer

✳ Ad

Euro

Sabon

Olive

dhand

cana

Lib

stile

Blippo

Countdown

From the late 1950s, the emergence of photocomposition technology created both a degree of uncertainty in the industry and an upsurge in the number of new typefaces being designed that could take advantage of the new technique. Typefaces that would have been almost impossible to produce with hot metal emerged as popular choices and played their own part in creating the signature looks of the decade.

Ad Lib
Freeman Craw | 1961

Antique Olive
Roger Excoffon | 1962–6

Eurostile
Aldo Novarese | 1962

Sabon
(Claude Garamond, 1500s)
Jan Tschichold | 1964–7

Americana
Richard Isbell | 1965

Countdown
Colin Brignall | 1965

Snell Roundhand
Matthew Carter | 1965

Hawthorn
Michael Daines | 1968

Syntax
Hans Eduard Meier | 1968

Blippo
Robert Trogman | 1969

Ad Lib

ABCDEFGHIJKLM
NOPQRSTUVWXYZ
abcdefghijklm
nopqrstuvwxyz
1234567890
(.,:;?!$£&-*){ÀÓÜÇ}

Ad Lib was designed by Freeman Craw for American Type Founders in 1961, and is very much a decorative display face, given that there is only one available weight. The combination of curves and rectangles in the letterforms strongly suggests a "woodcut" point of reference, while the jauntiness of the characters brings a cheerfully modern feel which looks surprisingly contemporary even today, although it works best when used to suggest retro styling. What this typeface does very well is evoke the feeling of a hand-drawn font without loss of quality. Novelty fonts are often badly drawn and only any good for nonprofessional use, but Ad Lib is an exception and is still a good choice for projects that require an injection of typographic humor.

Antique Olive

ABCDEFGHIJKLM
NOPQRSTUVWXYZ
abcdefghijklm
nopqrstuvwxyz
1234567890
(.,:;?!$£&-*){ÀÓÜÇ}

Antique Olive, designed by Roger Excoffon in 1962, is an odd fellow. It was commissioned by the French type foundry Fonderie Olive (hence the name, which does not in fact refer to the olive shape of the round characters) and was marketed as a more refined alternative to the then ubiquitous Helvetica. It is certainly an unusual typeface with its helping of Gallic charm, and the font is difficult to categorize with its sensual curves and very large x-height, but it works very well when used to conjure up a 1960s feel for text setting and demonstrates a high degree of legibility. To clarify a second misconception, the Antique in the name does not mean "old" in this instance—Antique was at the time used as the equivalent term for "sans-serif."

Countdown

ABCDEFGHIJKLM

NOPQRSTUVWXYZ

abcdefghijklm

nopqrstuvwxyz

1234567890

(.,:;?!$£&-*){ÀÓÜÇ}

Countdown was designed by Colin Brignall in 1965 and has the distinction of being the first original typeface to be designed exclusively for dry-transfer lettering company Letraset. Brignall was creative director of Letraset for many years and the company was responsible for shaping the look of display setting and for reinvigorating the fun side of typeface design for the next decade or so. The "spacey" look of the font found favor with scores of designers who needed to create a futuristic or computerized feel for their projects, and consequently its use reached saturation point quickly, which helps to bolster its reputation as one of "the" typefaces that sum up the 60s so well. It still looks good on a retro-styled club-night flyer or event poster. The sample shown is the Elsner+Flake version which attempts to replicate the original as closely as possible.

Sabon

ABCDEFGHIJKLM

NOPQRSTUVWXYZ

abcdefghijklm

nopqrstuvwxyz

1234567890

(.,:;?!$£&-*) {ÀÓÜÇ}

Sabon was designed by the great typographer Jan Tschichold between 1964 and 1967 to answer to a brief to design a typeface that would look the same in print regardless of how it was produced: by hand-composited foundry type, or with hot metal from both the Monotype and Linotype systems. The project was also to take text photosetting into account later in the 1970s when its use became more widespread. It was a major challenge as each system relies on different body widths (the width of each character) and the Linotype system made no allowance for kerning, or adjusting the spacing between individual characters. However, the design was extremely successful and the face is still widely used to this day. The design is derived from a slightly condensed cut of Garamond.

The price of the magazine is set in a typeface reminiscent of **Victorian** woodblock printing, a styling technique favored by both Pop Art and psychedelic-influenced graphic design.

The content notes are set in **Helvetica**, the typeface which arguably represents the International Style more than any other. *Oz* was always produced under severe budgetary constraints and Helvetica would have been a readily available typeface which every printer and typesetter would hold, due to its popularity as the most specified typeface of the 1960s and 1970s.

The photographic image of the topless female figure with overlaid type distorted to fit within the shape of her upper body suggests a link to the visual tricks used in the psychedelic concert posters designed by the likes of **Wes Wilson** (see pages 152–3) or **Victor Moscoso** (see page 146).

The collaged military comic-strip imagery directly references the paintings of **Roy Lichtenstein**, an artist whose work had become increasingly popular since the beginning of the decade.

Oz Magazine, Issue 8 Cover

Jon Goodchild & Virginia Clive-Smith | 1968

Oz magazine, the brainchild of Australians Richard Neville and Martin Sharp, published its first British edition in 1967. Essentially a satirical lifestyle magazine, *Oz* generally adopted an antiestablishment approach to its articles in support of 1960s counterculture and was federated to the movement known as the "underground press." Sharp filled the role of art director and was responsible for the overall design of each issue, but covers were sometimes produced in collaboration with others. The cover of Issue 8 which published in January 1968 was designed by Jon Goodchild and Virginia Clive-Smith and is a mishmash of typographic and illustrative styles in vogue at the time. Essentially Pop Art-influenced, the collage-style illustration also manages to reference psychedelia with the addition of the topless female figure in the background.

The editors of the magazine were famously charged with obscenity and brought to trial in 1971, accused with "conspiracy to corrupt public morals." They were subsequently acquitted following an appeal which revealed serious flaws in the procedure of the original trial.

The color palette row below is a sampler of colors selected from the *Oz* magazine cover shown here and is representative of the range of colors a designer working in this style might have used during the 1960s.

c = 000%	000%	000%	070%	080%	080%	080%	000%
m = 090%	070%	010%	010%	015%	000%	075%	070%
y = 080%	070%	100%	100%	045%	015%	000%	000%
k = 000%	000%	000%	000%	000%	000%	000%	000%

1970s

The 1960s 'Summer of Love' was well and truly over by the 1970s, but the newly politicized and socially aware generations that came of age remained vocal on the issues that mattered. The advancement of women's rights took a leap forward; in the UK the first Sex Discrimination Act came into force in 1975 along with the Equal Pay Act, and in the U.S. the Equal Rights Amendment gained ground rapidly although it did not receive full state ratification by its 1982 deadline. Also, in 1975, U.S. forces finally withdrew from Vietnam in the face of massive public opposition to a war which had lasted for eighteen years.

In economic terms the decade was the worst since the Great Depression of the 1930s, with high inflation and unemployment rife within the industrialized nations. For graphic designers, this pivotal decade saw further rapid development in the areas of design technology and typesetting. Phototypesetting, which had emerged during the 1960s, was constantly being improved and the technology was able to expand to smaller users when Compugraphic produced a range of affordable machines that for the first time allowed publishers to begin to set their own type to a professional standard. Pop Art and Psychedelia (see pages 144–7), so closely associated with the 1960s lifestyle, were more or less over at the beginning of the decade but, for a while at least, the International Style still held the high ground.

Postmodernism and New Wave typography

From the mid-1960s onward the dominance of the International Style experienced a gradual decline as designers became increasingly interested in the libertarianism of a movement termed "Postmodernism." This is not to say that Modernist design styles were abandoned; as we know, the International Style is still widely referenced along with other important twentieth century design styles.

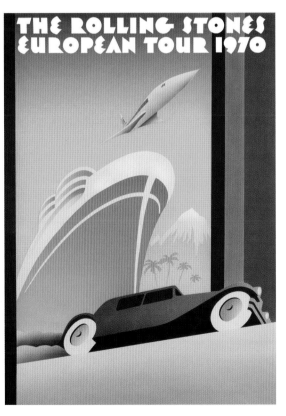

However, beginning with Pop Art and Psychedelia, a preference for the clean, organized layout and typography of the 1940s and 1950s was supplemented by an increase in the use of illustration over photography and a freer approach to typeface choices and stylistic form.

Postmodernism exists as a movement largely because an emancipated generation of artists and designers felt compelled to challenge the cultural hegemony enforced by the strict rules of the International Style.

Postmodernism is arguably the most overly debated and confusing term applied to any of the art and design movements described in this book. Essentially it is exactly what it says it is, a term created to describe what followed Modernism, the umbrella term used to describe the period running from the late nineteenth century through the first half of the twentieth. There is of course much more to it than that. To be more precise, Postmodernism rejects the central tenet of many Modernist styles—a master set of rules or theories which define everything about the style to which they are applied. Postmodernism is far more open-ended in its approach to graphic design style and does not attempt to corral a style by enforcing visual convention. It is important to stress that Postmodernism exists alongside Modernism; it does not advocate a completely different approach but rather it sets out to question and deconstruct the ideas behind Modernist design styles. It supports the philosophy that graphic design does not have to look the way it does simply because an established set of

Above left *Perhaps the most recognizable band logo of all time, The Rolling Stones "Lips" logo was designed by John Pasche in the Pop Art style in 1970 after Mick Jagger visited his degree show at the Royal College of Art in London.* © **Musidor BV**

Left *Pasche was also commissioned to design the band's European Tour poster in the same year, for which the inspiration is distinctly Art Deco.* © **John Pasche**

Above *A magazine cover for* Typografische Monatsblätter *designed by Dan Friedman in 1971. Friedman had previously been influenced by Wolfgang Weingart whilst he was studying at the Basel School of Design in Switzerland.*

pointers. Mixed typefaces used in a number of different point sizes and weights, disjointed and deconstructed approaches to layout structure, vernacular points of reference, and the deliberate inclusion of what appear to be errors in the execution of a piece are all Postmodernist earmarks. When used together or in isolation, all these points contradict the dogmatic guidelines of the International Style; with Postmodernism it is more a case of "If it feels right then it is right." In historical terms, Dada (see page 47) is arguably the nearest comparative style with its use of collage and mixed media and its anti-establishment stance.

There are several notable designers considered to be key postmodernist innovators. Wolfgang Weingart, a German designer and teacher, is credited as the inspiration behind the Postmodern style known as New Wave or Swiss Punk typography. He was one of the first designers to suggest that the International Style had reached a point where it was so prevalent it had become a style without drive or vision and taught his students to "view typography from all angles" and to consider that "type may be set centre axis, ragged left or right, perhaps sometimes in chaos." It is important to note that he was not instructing his students to totally ignore the rules of the International Style but rather to reevaluate how they could better inform fresh ideas about typography and layout. Dan Friedman and April Greiman (see pages 192–3), two of Weingart's students who had visited the Basel School of Design in Switzerland where he taught, would themselves go on to become important innovators, helping to introduce New Wave typography in the U.S.

visual guidelines says it should, and champions the view that design sensibilities are formed by social perception and therefore cannot be set in stone.

By its very nature the Postmodern look is difficult to define, but it is possible to provide some visual

Punk

Punk began as a music genre that emerged in the mid-1970s in the U.K., U.S., and to a lesser extent Australia. Although the traditional image of punk is firmly rooted in the London scene that began when the Sex Pistols played their first gig at Saint Martin's School of Art in 1975, the movement started in New York a year earlier when rock bands such as The New York Dolls, The Ramones, and artists such as Patti Smith would gather at the CBGB club in lower Manhattan. In terms of graphic design style, Punk is arguably the most extreme visual embodiment of Postmodernism with a DIY ethos that perfectly captured the spirit of punk culture and indeed the antiestablishment stance of younger generations at that time.

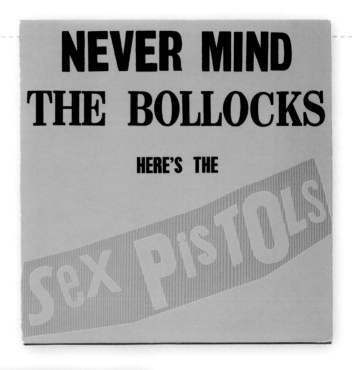

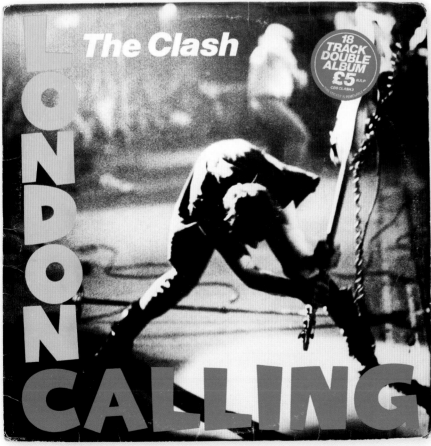

Above *The iconic sleeve designed by Jamie Reid for the Sex Pistols' only studio album* Never Mind the Bollocks, Here's the Sex Pistols, *released in October 1977.*

Left *The cover of* London Calling *by The Clash was designed by Ray Lowry in 1979 and features a photograph of bassist Paul Simonon taken by Pennie Smith at The Palladium in New York City. In true Postmodern style the typography echoes that of Elvis Presley's self-titled debut album.*

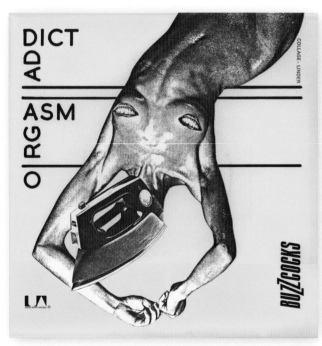

The Sex Pistols' manager Malcolm McLaren enlisted the help of his friend Jamie Reid (see pages 174–5) to create the artwork for the band's early releases and much of the subsequent punk style was drawn from those record sleeves. Ransom-note-style typography and roughly assembled collage artwork, often printed with a Day-Glo or garish color palette, became the de facto look for punk record covers and the main point of reference for many professional and amateur designers during the late 1970s. As mentioned above, the lack of structured grids, mixed typefaces in varying point sizes, and the link to the historic roots of Dadaism are what makes punk a thoroughly Postmodern design style.

Punk style did nonetheless possess a slightly more sophisticated edge which can be seen in the work of designers such as Barney Bubbles (real name Colin Fulcher) and Malcolm Garrett. Fulcher had worked as a senior designer for the Conran Group before beginning his freelance career working principally on commissions for the music industry. He designed a series of sleeves for British rock group Hawkwind before joining Stiff Records in 1977 as designer and art director. It was here that he created his best-known work for bands such as The Damned, Elvis Costello, and Ian Dury and the Blockheads before moving on to work at F-Beat Records. Sadly, suffering from depression and with financial worries, Barney Bubbles committed suicide in London in 1983.

Early in his career Malcolm Garrett designed a number of covers for the Buzzcocks including the iconic 1977 single release *Orgasm Addict* which features work by illustrator Linder Sterling. The typography is reminiscent of the International Typographic Style, while the overlaid collage references Pop Art and Dada. Other clients included Magazine, Duran Duran, Simple Minds, and Peter Gabriel. As an aside, Garrett was also one of the first British designers to embrace the new digital technology and his London studio was almost totally digital by 1990.

Top *Barney Bubbles' 1978 cover for the Ian Dury and the Blockheads single* Hit Me With Your Rhythm Stick.

Above *Malcolm Garrett's 1977 sleeve design for* Orgasm Addict *by the Buzzcocks featuring a collage by Linder Sterling.*

The ITC and *U&lc* magazine

The International Typeface Corporation, commonly referred to as the ITC, was formed in 1970 by designers Herb Lubalin (see pages 156–7) and Aaron Burns, and Ed Rondthaler of New York typesetting firm Photo-Lettering Inc. It was one of the first companies to license typefaces to third-party publishers and typesetting companies, a business model which is now very common, and was partly a reaction to the prevailing problem of typeface piracy. Revenue was dependent on how well each of the growing library of typefaces performed, so a promotional vehicle was required. The magazine *U&lc* (an abbreviation of "upper and lower case"), designed and art-directed by Lubalin until his death in 1981, was first published in 1973 and quickly became the most important magazine of its kind for graphic designers all over the world. A quarterly produced as a large-format tabloid and printed in a single color on newsprint, the magazine provided a regular source of information about the latest typeface releases in a pre-internet world and was hugely popular and influential. The popularity of typefaces would change with each issue; if a particular face was featured it would likely trend for the next few months before another issue was made available. *U&lc* ceased publication in 1999 and original copies are now considered collectors' items.

Hipgnosis

Looking at the images included in this chapter, one might think that practically all graphic design produced during the 1970s found its home on a record cover. This is not the case, but graphics and illustration created for albums and music posters during this period arguably reflect the design sensibilities and trends of the decade more than any other area. Of all the individual designers and consultancies active within the music industry during the 1970s there is one group that stands out more than any other because of its groundbreaking concepts and innovation: Hipgnosis.

The partnership formed in 1968 when the British band Pink Floyd asked Storm Thorgerson and Aubrey Powell to design the cover for their second studio album *A Saucerful of Secrets*. Thorgerson knew band members Syd Barrett and Roger Waters from his school days in Cambridge and was also a friend of

guitarist David Gilmour. Following a number of subsequent commissions from EMI the partnership acquired studio space in London's famous Denmark Street, known for its plethora of musical instrument stores and the 12 Bar Club live music venue, and went on to create some of the most memorable album covers of the late twentieth century. The duo were joined by designer Peter Christopherson in 1974—he began as an assistant and later became a partner.

The name Hipgnosis was derived from a piece of graffiti discovered by Thorgerson and Powell which, to quote Thorgerson, they liked because it possessed "a nice sense of contradiction, of an impossible coexistence, from Hip = new, cool, and groovy, and Gnostic, relating to ancient learning." In terms of house style, the approach generally favored photography over illustration and often incorporated the latest techniques for photographic manipulation

to enhance their sense of surrealism and love of visual puns. In a pre-Photoshop world these effects were achieved using elaborate darkroom techniques using multiple exposures, overlays and optical distortion, and airbrush retouching.

The pinnacle of Hipgnosis's achievements, or at least the most famous of their creations, is probably the cover of Pink Floyd's *The Dark Side of the Moon* which was conceived in collaboration with designer and illustrator George Hardie in 1973. Hardie was one of Hipgnosis's most frequent collaborators and the image has been reproduced millions of times, becoming one of the most iconic visuals to emerge from the 1970s. Other well-known bands that commissioned album covers from Hipgnosis between 1968 and 1983 include T. Rex, The Pretty Things, UFO,

10cc, Bad Company, Led Zeppelin, AC/DC, Scorpions, Yes, Def Leppard, Paul McCartney & Wings, The Alan Parsons Project, Genesis, Peter Gabriel, ELO, Rainbow, Styx, XTC, and Al Stewart. After Hipgnosis was dissolved in 1983 Thorgerson, Powell, and Christopherson formed music video production company Greenback Film, shooting promos for many of their existing clients over the next two years until the firm's closure. Powell continues to work in film production and direction, and stage set design. Thorgerson formed StormStudios with Peter Curzon in the early 90s as a freelance collective and continued to work on album covers and publishing projects until his death in 2013, despite suffering a stroke in 2003 which left him partially paralyzed.

Above The Dark Side of the Moon *by Pink Floyd, one of the most recognizable record covers of all time. It was designed by Storm Thorgerson and Aubrey Powell with illustration by George Hardie in 1973.*

Opposite Elegy *by The Nice was the band's final release in 1971 and features a photograph of fifty red footballs receding in a line into the dunes of the Sahara desert. It remains one of Hipgnosis's most recognizable cover images.*

Paula Scher

Paula Scher was born in Virginia in 1948 and studied at the Tyler School of Art in Philadelphia where she graduated in 1970 with a degree in fine art. After graduation, a relocation to New York provided her with her first job in the children's book division at publisher Random House, which was followed soon after in 1972 by a move to the advertising and promotions department at CBS Records. If this introduction to music graphics had not happened, Scher's career might have taken a different direction, but in 1974 she was offered the job of art director at Atlantic, a competitor of CBS. She stayed for just one year before returning to CBS where, over a period of eight years, she designed over one hundred and fifty record covers, earning no less than four Grammy nominations in the process.

Scher is a prime example (as are many of the other individuals profiled in this book) of a designer that is difficult to place in one particular decade. At the time of writing she is a Pentagram partner based at the New York office—incidentally the first woman to become a partner—and is still creating groundbreaking graphic design. However, the work she produced during the period from 1975 to 1982 is particularly significant because of the way it influenced record cover design throughout the 70s and 80s, and because of the way the record-buying public connected with the visuals. Bear in mind that at this time the record covers themselves were collectable in the same way that poster collecting had been popularized during the previous decade. Fans would often make an album purchasing decision based on the cover as well as the musical content, purely to be completist, so covers were so much more important than they are today. Scher's famous cover for the band Boston, designed with illustrator Roger Huyssen in 1976, provides us with an image that sums up 1970s graphic style perfectly and synchs with the penchant for science-fiction themes which were prevalent throughout the decade. Scher herself has since quipped that she is "horrified" by the idea that she may be remembered as the "art director of the original Boston album." Other classic CBS pieces include Eric Gale's *Ginseng Woman* with illustration by David Wilcox, and her 1979 Best of Jazz promotional poster designed as a Constructivist word cloud.

swatch◻

Scher's work during this period and after also clearly identifies her as a pioneer of the Postmodern movement as she would often draw her influences from a variety of different styles and was comfortable with the idea of appropriation, a key component of Postmodern design style. Her 1985 recreation of Herbert Matter's 1936 Constructivist *Winterferien— doppelte Ferien, Schweiz* poster as a magazine advertisement for Swatch is a perfect example. In 1984 she cofounded Koppel & Scher with fellow designer Terry Koppel before becoming a Pentagram partner in 1991. Her best-known work in more recent years includes the Constructivist-style typographic compositions for The Public Theater in New York, and her hand-painted typographic maps.

Jamie Reid

Born in Belfast in 1947, Jamie Reid grew up in London and is known as the foremost graphic designer of the British punk era of the 1970s and early 1980s. His importance as a graphic designer lies not only in the work produced during that period for Malcolm McLaren and the Sex Pistols, but also as one of the principal originators of a style that swept away many of the pretensions that had become associated with graphic design and with art, opening the door to a brand new and totally anarchistic visual sensibility that would both change and inform the way graphic design was perceived over the following decades.

Reid trained as a painter at Croydon School of Art in South London from 1964 to 1968, acquiring a deep interest in left-wing politics at the same time. After graduating he became involved with the Situationists, a French-based Marxist group, and cofounded the Suburban Press which published material for left-wing political groups, anarchists, and women's groups from 1970 to 1975. With funds presumably in short supply, it was here that Reid first began to develop his photomontage style of hand-cut graphics and ransom-note-style typography using letters cut from existing printed material, Letraset, and handwritten script.

By the mid-seventies British Punk was gearing up to full speed, in line with the disaffectedness of a bored generation of youths with no jobs, no hope, and

no future (a phrase soon appropriated for a certain well-known punk anthem). Malcolm McLaren, punk entrepreneur and friend of Reid from their days at Croydon School of Art, had achieved some success with the Kings Road clothes store SEX that he ran with his partner Vivienne Westwood, and following his rather less successful stint promoting rock band The New York Dolls in the U.S. he was ready to try again in Britain. In the summer of 1975 he took a group of regular customers under his wing and persuaded them to form the Sex Pistols. McLaren approached Reid to design promotional posters and T-shirts for the band, and the graphic style he had begun to develop at Suburban Press was deemed perfect for the burgeoning Punk scene.

Reid's first promotional poster for the Sex Pistols, *Anarchy in the UK* single release in 1976 featured a ripped-up Union Jack flag held together with safety pins, a motif borrowed from the fashion statements echoed in the clothing sold at McLaren's store.

The even more famous covers for the singles *God Save the Queen*, *Pretty Vacant*, and the iconic album cover of *Never Mind the Bollocks, Here's the Sex Pistols*, came to symbolize Punk style, and Reid would go on to create many more pieces of Punk "art" before the movement fragmented into the various subcultures which would help define 1980s style.

Reid continues to work as a politically motivated artist and in 2011 staged an exhibition of his work in north London entitled "Ragged Kingdom."

Above *The sleeve for* Pretty Vacant, *designed by Reid in 1977, takes a slightly more sophisticated approach than other Sex Pistols covers of the time but still features the ransom-note-style typography.*

Opposite *The 7-inch single sleeve of* God Save the Queen *by the Sex Pistols, featuring a Dadaesque collage of Queen Elizabeth II. 1977 was the year of the Queen's sliver jubilee, a fact which helped promote the notoriety of the record and the band considerably.*

ITC Avant Gard

Fat Face

ITC

Frutiger

ITC Serif G

Bell Cente

ITC Friz Qu

ITC Benguiat

American Ty

Gothic

Galliard

othic

nnial*

adrata

Gothic

pewriter

Zapf Chancery

The 1970s represent a turning point in type design; photocomposition technology all but replaced hot-metal setting and in turn created a kind of renaissance moment for type designers where newly formed typeface manufacturers and distributors were keen to invest in new typeface designs which they could market exclusively. The International Typeface Corporation (see page 169) was hugely influential during this period and the typical typographic styling of the decade is largely a result of the faces distributed by them.

ITC Avant Garde Gothic
Herb Lubalin, Tom Carnase | 1970

ITC Fat Face
Herb Lubalin, Tom Carnase | 1970

ITC Friz Quadrata
Ernst Friz, Victor Caruso | 1973

American Typewriter
Joel Kaden, Tony Stan | 1974

ITC Serif Gothic
Herb Lubalin, Tony Dispigna | 1974

Frutiger
Adrian Frutiger | 1976

Bell Centennial
Matthew Carter | 1978

ITC Benguiat Gothic
Ed Benguiat | 1978

Galliard
Matthew Carter | 1978

Zapf Chancery
Hermann Zapf | 1979

American Typewriter

ABCDEFGHIJKLM
NOPQRSTUVWXYZ
abcdefghijklm
nopqrstuvwxyz
1234567890
(.,:;?!$£&-*){ÀÓÜÇ}

American Typewriter was designed for ITC in 1974 by Joel Kaden and Tony Stan to provide a typeface that would emulate the character forms and monospaced style of the classic Sholes's typewriter font. Monospacing is a practical solution implemented on regular mechanical typewriters where every character occupies the same horizontal space, thus allowing the type bars to be equally sized too. American Typewriter retains the personality of genuine typewritten text and is a friendlier alternative to the more impersonal Courier designed by Howard Kettler in 1955. Its best-known appearance is probably as the typeface used in Milton Glaser's famous "I heart NY" logo of 1977.

ITC Friz Quadrata

ABCDEFGHIJKLM
NOPQRSTUVWXYZ
abcdefghijklm
nopqrstuvwxyz
1234567890
(.,:;?!$£&-*){ÀÓÜÇ}

ITC Friz Quadrata is the commercial release of the typeface designed originally in 1973 by Ernst Friz and Victor Caruso for Visual Graphics Corporation. The International Typeface Corporation (ITC) came on board a little later when the family was expanded to include a bold weight. Friz Quadrata has proved to be an incredibly popular typeface choice for logo designers over the years, particularly in the case of educational institutions and universities, and for other applications where a degree of seriousness can be combined with an injection of personality. This glyphic serif-style typeface with its hand-carved aesthetic lends itself well to this usage as it displays the right balance of classic styling with a touch of modernity to carry it off.

Frutiger

ABCDEFGHIJKLM
NOPQRSTUVWXYZ
abcdefghijklm
nopqrstuvwxyz
1234567890
(.,:;?!$£&-*){ÀÓÜÇ}

In 1968, Paris's newly built Charles de Gaulle International Airport commissioned Swiss typeface designer Adrian Frutiger to design a typeface for use on all its signage systems. The new face had to be highly legible from a distance and needed to be flexible enough to work in a wide variety of point sizes. The eponymously named Frutiger is based in part on his previous triumph Univers, and takes additional influences from the calligraphic letterforms of humanist sans-serif type. Despite the fact that Frutiger was designed for signage it succeeds very well as a text face when used at small point sizes, a fact that has contributed to the typeface's enduring popularity as a no-nonsense workhorse. The commercial release of Frutiger came in 1976 via the D. Stempel AG foundry.

Bell Centennial

ABCDEFGHIJKLM
NOPQRSTUVWXYZ
abcdefghijklm
nopqrstuvwxyz
1234567890
(.,:;?!$£&-*){ÀÓÜÇ}

In part to celebrate its one-hundredth birthday, and to improve the legibility of its printed telephone directories, the American Telephone and Telegraph Company (AT&T) asked Matthew Carter to design a new typeface to address the limitations of Bell Gothic which had been used since 1937. Introduced in 1978, Bell Centennial included four styles instead of the two offered by Bell Gothic and was designed to be legible when printed in 6-point on low-grade paper. The styles are sympathetically labeled Name and Number, Address, Bold Listing, and Sub-Caption. The sample shown here is Name and Number, one of the bolder styles which include ink traps—small notches cut into characters where stems and strokes join. These prevent excess ink gathering at these points during printing and preserve the true shape of the characters.

Die Mensch-Maschine (The Man Machine)

Emil Schult | 1978

Over the years a number of important bands have gone to great lengths to ensure that their graphics are closely linked to their music, but German band Kraftwerk are arguably the most vociferous practitioners of this approach. Ralf Hütter and Florian Schneider released the first Kraftwerk album in 1970, and from the beginning have ensured that both their musical and visual output have remained inseparable. The designer Emil Schult has been involved in practically all Kraftwerk covers and even became the band's guitarist briefly during 1973 until the emphasis on synthesizer-based music meant a guitar was no longer required. Schult also co-wrote the lyrics for *The Model*, the bands most successful 7″ single release.

The cover of *Die Mensch-Maschine* (The Man-Machine) is heavily influenced by the work of El Lissitzky (see page 53) with the reverse of the cover designed as an homage of sorts to his book *Of Two Squares*. El Lissitzky's typographic style was influenced strongly by De Stijl as well as Constructivism and the De Stijl style is reflected in the main typography of the sleeve. El Lissitzsky was also a frequent visitor to the Bauhaus (see page 68) where a principle aim was the reestablishment of a unity between the applied arts and technology, highly appropriate for a synth-band.

The color palette row below is a sampler of colors selected from the album sleeve shown here, plus some supplementary colors, and is representative of the range of colors a designer working in this style might have used during the 1970s.

The cover's main typography is reminiscent of a constructivist approach but also displays strong links with De Stijl, a movement which El Lissitzky participated in during the 1920s.

The bold black and red color scheme with hints of green and brown is strongly reminiscent of a typical constructivist color palette. The band's trademark anonymity is expressed through the identical clothing worn by the members.

The album's title is also shown in Russian, German, and French, which underscores the internationalism of the band's music. The language used to display the main title at top left was rotated according the territory in which the album was released.

c =	030%	040%	055%	015%	000%	025%	000%	000%
m =	015%	025%	035%	025%	080%	080%	090%	000%
y =	030%	040%	050%	040%	070%	085%	090%	000%
k =	000%	000%	020%	000%	000%	010%	000%	100%

1980s

The 1980s heralded a new age of technological advancement alongside a significant "boom and bust" economic period which resonates with the global recession experienced once again during the late 2000s and early 2010s. At the beginning of the decade, digital technology still felt like an unachievable and unaffordable dream but by the early 1990s many graphic designers would find themselves sitting in front of a computer instead of a drawing board.

We witnessed the advent of the video game, the rise of the Sony Walkman, the VHS video cassette winning out over the technologically superior Betamax, and a new period of space exploration with America's space shuttle program. Most significantly for the graphic design industry, the Apple Macintosh was announced in 1984 during the third-quarter break of Super Bowl XVIII with the now famous Chiat/Day (now TBWA\ Chiat\Day since a 1995 merger) produced *1984* advertisement directed by Ridley Scott.

The decade will of course also be remembered for big shoulder pads, big hair, and countless other questionable trends best consigned to the fashion history books. However, in terms of advancing the profile of graphic design as an important cultural compass, the decade is second to none.

The rise of the style magazine

The golden age of magazines is often identified as a period which ended during the 1950s when Alexey Brodovitch was art director at *Harper's Bazaar*, but the 1980s witnessed the ascendancy of a new kind of magazine which perfectly personifies a decade somewhat obsessed with style. Style magazines presented a new kind of platform for the dissemination of information to a generation of

THE FACE No. 42   ● OCTOBER 1983 75p

THE FACE

BODY AND SOUL

THE HIDD∈N FACE OF FANTASY SEX
IN THE MIX : SEARCHING FOR N.Y.'S PERFECT BEAT
EXCLUSIVE : INSIDE FIORUCCI'S PRIVATE MUSEUM

ANNIE LENNOX UNMASKED · JAMIE REID · BRIAN ENO
GWEN GUTHRIE · MEL GIBSON · CUSTOM SCOOTERS

portfolio—the style magazines provided readers with a collection of features designed to provide the inside knowledge on fashion, music, film, and sport presented as entertainment rather than simply a source of information. Mainstream magazine publishing relied traditionally on revenue from advertising to generate profits for the publishing house, but this new brand of magazine was much more about maintaining a contiguous high-quality design style from cover to cover. To ensure this was achieved, potential advertisers that did not make a good fit with the image of the magazine were sometimes turned away, the preference being to ditch the revenues rather than run the risk of alienating the readership.

The two stand-out style magazines from the early 1980s were *The Face* and *i-D*, both of which launched in London in 1980. The editor of *The Face*, Nick Logan, had previously cut his teeth at the weekly music newspaper *New Musical Express* and had created the successful music magazine *Smash Hits*. He appointed Neville Brody (see pages 188–9) as designer and art director of *The Face* in 1981. Brody's innovative approach to typographic headline devices and layouts struck an immediate chord with the visually aware

fashion-conscious readers, hungry for the facts about the freshest trends, the coolest clubs, and the hippest music.

One of the principal distinctions of the magazines of this genre that emerged in the 1980s was the way they challenged the assumptions about content and magazine design philosophy. To begin—that is to say before the rebellious edge to this style of magazine publishing gave way to a more commercialized model—the editors and designers felt compelled to dismiss normal conventions in order to attract a particular type of reader who would instantly understand the editorial direction, vernacular references, and cutting-edge styling of the magazine content. Like monthly "look books"—the term used to describe a photographer's or fashion label's bound

On the cover:
WINTER '86/'87 DECEMBER/JANUARY £1.40 FROM THE PUBLISHERS OF THE FACE

ARENA
132 PAGES
A NEW MAGAZINE FOR MEN

ISSUE ONE: A cover for Mickey Rourke/ Rich Girls! What else can a poor boy do?/Walter Matthau slices the cake/The Art Racket/John Lahr talks Joe Orton/ Mike Tyson hits where it hurts/ Rock climbing: Man at the top/46 pages of men's FASHION A1

ARENA FASHION: ITALIAN AND BRITISH SUITS, CASHMERE AND LEVIS, WINTER COATS, CASUAL JACKETS

Above Arena magazine launched in 1986 with Neville Brody as its first art director. The magazine was published continuously for 22 years but folded in 2009 under pressure from the plethora of other men's magazines that emerged after Arena's original publication.

readership; his preference for Russian Constructivism (see pages 62–5) as one his principal influences caused a revival in the use of the style, and his brand of graphic design was much imitated throughout the decade. As a very public platform with a high circulation, *The Face* was the vehicle by which Brody himself and Postmodern graphic design in general were brought to the attention of a mass audience. Brody left his position to art-direct another Logan-backed project, men's style magazine *Arena*, in 1986, and *The Face* finally ceased publication in 2004.

i-D magazine launched in the same year with Terry Jones, former art director of British *Vogue*, at the helm. The first issue was intentionally Lo-Fi, taking the form of a hand-crafted fanzine with a DIY look, and the design of interior spreads in the earlier issues displayed a highly deconstructed aesthetic. Jones liked to push the boundaries of legibility as far as possible—his approach to art direction is distinctly postmodern, carrying many of the hallmark features that became associated with 1980s editorial design.

i-D content policy differed from *The Face* in that it placed a greater emphasis on street fashion over high-end designer chic. It pioneered a style of portrait photography which was part fashion, part documentary, and became known as "The Straight Up." The subjects were often fashionable people spotted on the streets of London rather than professional models, and were simply photographed standing against the nearest available backdrop. The deconstructed approach has been tempered over the years in line with a return to a modernist revival look, but the edginess remains to this day.

i-D

STARRING:
CAPRICORN
AQUARIUS
PISCES
ARIES
TAURUS
GEMINI
CANCER
LEO
VIRGO
LIBRA
SCORPIO
SAGITTARIUS
▼

ALL STAR

Left i-D *magazine launched with a DIY-style fanzine aesthetic but quickly adapted to a more sophisticated look aligned more closely to other style and fashion magazines being published in the early 1980s.* **Photography Nick Knight, i-D, The All Star Issue, No. 14, April 83**

Below *The first spread from issue No.1 of i-D magazine to feature the "Straight Up" style of fashion photography.* **Photography Steve Johnston, i-D, No. 1, 1980**

COLIN: Mode - Colin is wearing black pleated trousers which he made himself. The cardigan is from Marks and Spencers, £9.99 and the shoes from Axiom in the Kings Road, £5.99. Fave music - Siouxsie and the Banshees and David Bowie.

WiLD i-D!

STRAIGHT UP

Photographed by Steve Johnston

Anonymous girl with spiky hair-do.

1980s

The three "A"s

In the mid-1980s three "A"s caused the biggest shake-up in the graphic design world since Linotype and Monotype introduced their linecasting and character casting machines a hundred years earlier. These 'A's were Apple, Adobe, and Aldus, and the coming together of each company's products provided graphic designers with a method of working that, previous to the introduction of the new technology, would have been completely impossible. The desktop publishing revolution had arrived and, as with all periods of major change, not everyone was happy about it.

In 1984 a small company based in California debuted a computer with, for its time, advanced graphics capabilities and a revolutionary user interface. The Apple Macintosh was expensive but initial sales were strong and the Mac captured the attention of graphic designers interested in innovation and new ways of working. At this stage it would be fair to say that many design professionals did not think typesetters and traditional art workers had too much too worry about. Roughly a year later, after sales had begun to flag due to the limited usage opportunities offered by this otherwise exceptional computer, another Californian company named Adobe launched PostScript, a page description language which allowed computers to create and print scalable vector graphics. These are images constructed from points, lines, curves, and shapes; each character in a PostScript typeface is an individual vector image.

In the same year Apple launched the LaserWriter, a PostScript-enabled desktop printer; and Washington-based software developer Aldus released Pagemaker, page-layout software that provided an art-working solution for graphic designers and typographers. It was Aldus's founder Paul Brainerd who first coined the phrase "desktop publishing." In style terms the effect on graphic design was not immediate as

Left *The Apple Macintosh has come an awfully long way since 1984. Apple's current Mac Pro desktop computer is capable of tasks that engineers could only dream of thirty years ago.* **Courtesy of Apple Inc.**

the equipment was still relatively expensive, but within a couple of years the built-in savings generated by not having to order-in typesetting helped to justify the investment—and it was then that objections began to emerge from the typographic establishment. The problem lay in the fact that high-quality typesetting had always been produced by experienced professionals with many years of experience, but now anyone who could acquire the kit could set their own type. In the same way that typographic standards suffered on the introduction of phototypesetting in the 1960s, some dreadful typographic crimes were committed by designers in the name of progress. This was partly down to inexperience on the part of the end-users, and partly because of the limitations of the technology in the early days, but if it were not for this side-effect the radical styling of the late 1980s and 1990s would not have emerged.

Thanks to progressive type designers like Rudy VanderLans and Zuzana Licko; designers such as Wolfgang Weingart, April Greiman (see pages 192–93), Neville Brody (see pages 188–89), and Erik Spiekermann; and enlightened educational establishments such as the Cranbrook Academy of Art in Michigan (see page 187); digital typography found its own niche as a deconstructive style that influenced the look of graphic design throughout the 1990s. Over time the hardware and software have improved, and fortunately the majority of professional graphic designers have become better typesetters too, allowing the design profession greater control over how it works and what it is able to create.

Cranbrook Academy of Art

Though it may seem odd to single out one art college when there are so many notable teaching establishments around the world Cranbrook, situated in Bloomfield Hills, Michigan, earns a mention because of its early support for New Wave typography and a Postmodern approach to graphic design tuition. Traditionally, graphic design education in Europe and the United States focused on preparing students for a career by teaching them about the rules which govern the International Style, and about professional practice. In 1971 graphic designer Katherine McCoy and her husband, industrial designer Michael McCoy, joined the teaching staff at Cranbrook. Katherine led the graphic design program and from the beginning was interested in trying to change the way the course was structured so a greater emphasis could be placed on experimentation and the need to fully express the meaning of design solutions, something which she considered more important than a strict adherence to visual boundaries and a requirement to pander to the needs of the design profession. In this masters program, the standard system of assignments and deadlines was modified to emphasize an open-ended arrangement where students were expected to self-initiate new work for regular weekly critiques and self-evaluate at the end of each semester. A final degree project and thesis were required for graduation.

The emphasis on experimentation and self-development is thoroughly Postmodern in its approach and was both revolutionary and controversial, but the success experienced by many Cranbrook graduates evidenced the effectiveness of McCoy's innovative approach which would go on to be adopted by other important schools such as Cal Arts under the

Above *A recruitment poster for Cranbrook designed by Katherine McCoy in 1989. The photographic collage in the background is composed of projects produced by Cranbrook students and the diagrammatic overlay hints at the experimental approach to teaching espoused by the college.*

directorship of Lorraine Wild. Visiting lecturers such as Wolfgang Weingart helped cement the school's reputation and the "Cranbrook style" became highly influential throughout the 1980s and beyond. The school is associated in particular with the emerging technology of digital graphic design and typography and the role many of its graduates played in the promotion of the new digital aesthetic. Selected Cranbrook graduates include Andrew Blauvelt, Elliott Earls, Edward Fella, Jeffery Keedy, P. Scott Makela, Nancy Skolos and Thomas Wedell, Lucille Tenazas, and Lorraine Wild.

Neville Brody

Neville Brody was born in London in 1957 and studied fine art at foundation level at the Hornsey College of Art before beginning a graphics degree at the LCP (London College of Printing) in 1976. He found the LCP to be somewhat stifling and was even accused by his tutors of producing "uncommercial" work, although Brody rejected this view on the basis that he felt ideas were more important than the potential commercial application for whatever he produced. The Punk scene was beginning to peak around this time and Brody, like many of his contemporaries, was influenced by the associated styles and energy of the Punk philosophy. However, he was at the same time drawn to a number of historical graphic styles from the 1920s and 1930s, particularly Dada and Russian Constructivism (see pages 62–5). He became a great admirer of the work of designers such as El Lissitzky (see page 53) and Alexander Rodchenko (see pages 72–3), and used their work as a point of reference when developing his own contemporary take on the style.

As the initial power of Punk waned and the post-Punk era began in earnest, Brody joined record label Rocking Russian as a sleeve designer immediately after his graduation. After nine months of what Brody described in his 1988 book *The Graphic Language of Neville Brody* (Thames & Hudson) as "absolute poverty" he moved to Stiff Records, then to Fetish Records where he stayed until 1981. It was at this point that Brody was appointed art director of the groundbreaking magazine *The Face*, first launched by publisher Nick Logan in May 1980, and it was largely on the basis of this move that he earned his reputation. Brody brought something completely new to magazine design during his six years at *The Face*, using his ability to draw from various sources such as street style and the more esoteric elements of American Mid-Century Modern to create a complete visual language using type and form. His attraction to Russian Constructivism also played a large part in the process and Brody created many custom typefaces and glyphs to use as headlines for articles in each separate issue. Most of the work was drawn by hand, but Brody was also interested in the emerging digital technology and began to use computers at an early

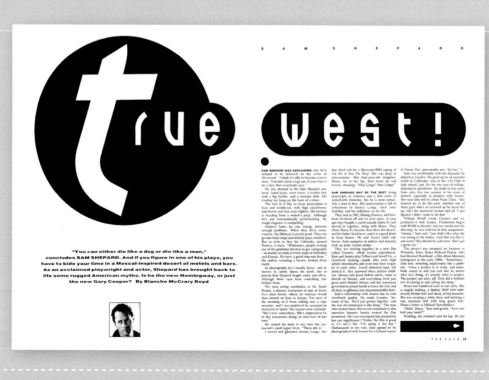

stage in the development of this new way of working. Several of his hand-drawn headlines from this period would eventually become full alphabets with a commercial release.

In 1986 Brody became art director of men's style magazine *Arena*, staying in the position until 1990. During the same period he launched his own practice, the Neville Brody Studio, which in 1994 became Research Studios, and his book for Thames & Hudson was accompanied by an exhibition at London's Victoria & Albert Museum. It was this particular accolade which propelled Brody to a status akin to that of a rock star in the design world, the first graphic designer to achieve this in the modern era.

In addition to the London office, Research Studios maintain a presence in Paris, Berlin, and Barcelona and specialize in the creation of unique visual languages across applications ranging from film and television to websites, packaging, and corporate identity. Brody was also a founding member of FontShop, a digital font foundry based in London, and of FontFont along with fellow designer Erik Spiekermann.

Above *The cover of 23 Skidoo's album* Just Like Everybody, *designed by Brody in 1987 and featuring a fine example of his custom lettering style.*

Below *Spreads from issue no. 59 of* The Face, *published in March 1985.*

Studio Dumbar

Dutch graphic designer Gert Dumbar was born in 1940 and studied graphic design and painting at the Royal Academy of Fine Arts in The Hague from 1959 to 1964 before moving to London to study typography at the Royal College of Art from 1964 to 1967. During his time at college his approach to his own design philosophy was greatly affected by the ideas of the contemporary art movement Fluxus which was conceived by the Lithuanian artist and designer George Maciunas during the 1960s. Fluxus considered the Dada artist Marcel Duchamp (see page 47) one of its principal influences and advocated a kind of "do-it-yourself" aesthetic with an anti-commercial sensibility, encouraging artists and designers to work with whatever they cared to appropriate in terms of either materials of influences. While still a student, Dumbar had experimented with and perfected a technique which he called staged photography. He would construct still-life arrangements from cut paper, papier-mâché solids, and other found objects, then have them photographed in front of backgrounds composed of collage or textured surfaces. Elements such as text or additional illustrated elements could then be added on an overlay to create the multilayered

posters and intricate overlaid typography which would subsequently become his studio's signature "look." The styling is compatible with a Postmodern approach as the resulting image would often require some degree of deciphering on the part of the viewer to comprehend its meaning.

He became Creative Director of the design group Tel Design in 1967 and worked primarily on corporate identity projects, claiming Dutch Railways as an important client in the process. Despite this success he found the strict commercial business model he was required to work with too restrictive, so left in 1977 to establish Studio Dumbar in The Hague. This allowed him greater freedom to choose projects with artistic merit; ironically, a formula which seemed to please his previous clients as many chose to continue working with him at the new business.

The internal structure adopted by Studio Dumbar from its beginning is famed for its flexibility, an arrangement the studio opts to term "controlled chaos." The system relies on designers working together on an equal footing, with teamwork and open dialogue considered an important component of the creative process. The studio is also known for providing many interns with their first taste of a professional design practice and from the 1980s it maintained close relationships with both the Royal College of Art and with Cranbrook Academy (see page 187) in Michigan. The studio's clients over the years have included Apple, Nike, Philips, Amsterdam's Rijksmuseum, and notably the PTT (Dutch Postal, Telegraph, and Telephone Authority) for which Studio Dumbar undertook one of the most ambitious corporate identity programs ever produced. In 2003 Gert Dumbar retired and the studio moved to Rotterdam under the creative direction of Michel de Boer, with additional offices opening in Shanghai (2005) and Seoul (2012). Since 2010 Studio Dumbar is led by Liza Enebeis (Creative Director), Karmen Kekic (Client Service Director) and Tom Dorresteijn (CEO and Strategy).

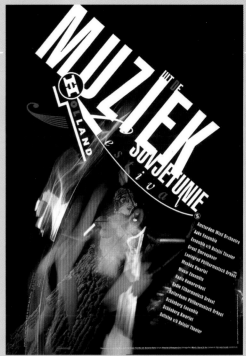

Above and right *Promotional posters and a program for the Holland Festival, the Netherlands' oldest and largest performing arts festival, which takes place every June in Amsterdam. The pieces were designed between 1987 to 1989. Design: Studio Dumbar; Photography: Lex van Pieterson.*
Images courtesy of Studio Dumbar

Opposite *The 1989 corporate identity manual for Koninklijke PTT Nederland, commissioned following the privatization of the Dutch Postal, Telegraph, and Telephone Authority. Design: Studio Dumbar; Photo: Gerrit Schreurs.*
Image courtesy of Studio Dumbar

April Greiman

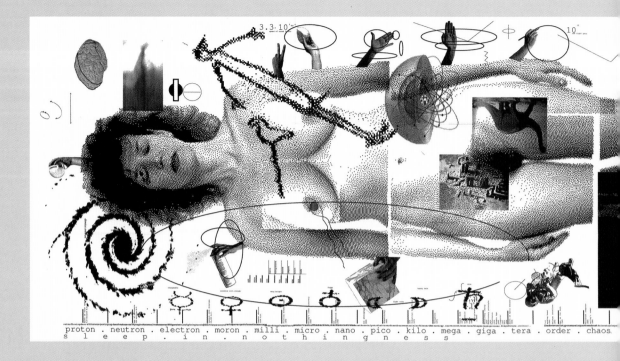

April Greiman began her career working as a graphic designer in NYC in the 1970s, having been born in Metropolitan New York in 1948. She studied at Kansas City Art Institute between 1966 and 1970 before spending a postgraduate year in Basel, Switzerland, at the Allgemeine Künstgewerbeschule. She was taught by Armin Hofmann and Wolfgang Weingart and was influenced by the International Style and by Weingart's developing style of New Wave typography, also known as Swiss Punk, which rejected the traditional elements of Modernism in favor of a more post-industrial approach. Greiman returned to New York but by 1976, being a restless creative spirit, she felt a change of scene was needed and relocated to Los Angeles. It was here that she began to develop her multidisciplinary approach to graphics, experimenting with techniques that both preceded and predicted the styles that would come out of the digital revolution that would begin several years later.

In her first job after moving west, Greiman hired designer and photographer Jayme Odgers to shoot a series of images and they went on to form a creative partnership that would last for several years, producing among other projects an influential poster for California Institute of the Arts in 1979, and a poster for the 1984 Olympics. By 1982 Greiman had been appointed Director of Graphic Design for CalArts, providing an opportunity for her to work with some of the most advance design technology available at the time. This period is particularly important in Greiman's career as it allowed her the time and resources to expand her multidisciplinary style by experimenting with state-of-the-art video paintbox equipment alongside an analog computer in the Film department during her spare time. The experience provided the first opportunity to integrate new technology into her work and Greiman realized that the way graphic design was created at the time was about to be turned on its head. In 1984 she returned to professional practice and bought a Mac.

What is arguably her most recognized piece of work from this period was created a couple of years later in 1986. *Design Quarterly*, published by the Walker Art Centre until 1993, invited Greiman to be

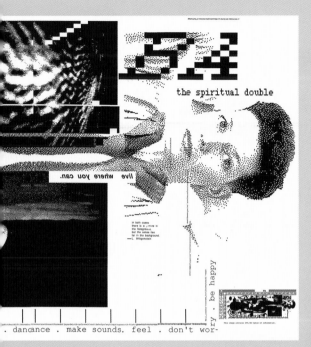

the subject of issue no. 133 and also to design it. She called the issue "Does It Make Sense?" and, instead of using the standard thirty-two page format, she produced the magazine as large-format fold-out poster measuring approximately three by six feet. The front pictured a naked self-portrait composed of digitized images overlaid with blocks of images and text, while the back featured a selection of video grabs interspersed with notations about digital technology. It was a considerable achievement at a time when the fledgling technology was barely usable and rendering and printing times were so slow that it could take a whole day to print a file. Prior to "Does It Make Sense?," the idea that a Mac could ever be a serious design tool was widely ridiculed, but attitudes changed after Greiman's poster appeared. It is because of this that April Greiman is considered one of the first pioneers of digital design. She currently runs her own Los Angeles-based practice, Made in Space.

Monotype

Matrix

Lucida Sans

ITC Usher

Arial *

ITC Stone

Rotis Semi

TYPEFACE

Calvert
TRAJAN
ood
Matrix
Serif
Serif
SIX

Digital typesetting arrived in the 1980s and once again available technology proved to be highly influential in terms of the choices made by type designers. Typically, the digital printers of the time were not capable of high-resolution output so typefaces that could cope with low-resolution output were designed specifically for the purpose. Deconstructed typography, and faces with a strong historical resonance, combined with a modern geometric aesthetic, characterize this decade.

Monotype Calvert
Margaret Calvert | 1980

Arial
Robin Nicholas, Patricia Saunders | 1982

ITC Usherwood
Les Usherwood | 1984

Lucida Sans
Charles Bigelow, Kris Holmes | 1985

Matrix
Zuzana Licko | 1986

Typeface Six
Neville Brody | 1986

ITC Stone Serif
Sumner Stone | 1987

Lunatix
Zuzana Licko | 1988

Rotis SemiSerif
Otl Aicher | 1988

Trajan
Carol Twombly | 1989

Arial

ABCDEFGHIJKLM
NOPQRSTUVWXYZ
abcdefghijklm
nopqrstuvwxyz
1234567890
(.,:;?!$£&-*){ÀÓÜÇ}

Arial is probably best known as the sans-serif typeface that is bundled with all releases of the Microsoft Windows and Apple Mac OSX operating systems. To that extent (and this is not meant in any way to sound condescending) non-designers have been known to use "Arial" as a general term for sans-serif type in the same way people call vacuum cleaners Hoovers. Because of its ubiquity it is sometimes avoided by professional designers but is nonetheless a very well-designed and useful typeface with an enormous range of styles and weights. It is very similar in proportion to Helvetica but features subtle differences such as a straight rather than curved leg on the "R". It was designed in 1982 by Robin Nicholas and Patricia Saunders for Monotype and first appeared as an installed font on the IBM 3800-3 laser printer.

ITC Stone Serif

ABCDEFGHIJKLM
NOPQRSTUVWXYZ
abcdefghijklm
nopqrstuvwxyz
1234567890
(.,:;?!$£&-*){ÀÓÜÇ}

The ITC Stone Serif family was the first style of a superfamily of typefaces designed by the then Adobe Director of Typography Sumner Stone in 1987. A number of projects looking at the ways different styles of typeface can be mixed within a single piece of design were inaugurated during the 1980s—with ITC Stone Serif being one of the higher-profile examples. ITC Stone Sans, ITC Stone Humanist, and ITC Stone Informal would eventually complete the set. The advantage of having different styles of typeface designed to form a specific group is provided by the consistent cap height and x-height, and by the consistent weights of the strokes and stems. Each style features three weights: medium, semibold, and bold.

Rotis Semi Serif

ABCDEFGHIJKLM
NOPQRSTUVWXYZ
abcdefghijklm
nopqrstuvwxyz
1234567890
(.,:;?!$£&-*){ÀÓÜÇ}

Like the Stone family of typefaces discussed on the previous page, Rotis was drawn in 1988 in four flavors by German designer Otl Aicher as an experiment to see how a unified type family with both serif and sans-serif options could work when used in combination. His goal was to create different styles that would all display an even tone (typographers refer to this tone as typographic color) of gray, thus allowing the use of one style for headings, one for text, another for captions, and so on in a visually harmonious way. The styles consist of Rotis Serif, Rotis Semi Serif (shown here), Rotis Semi Sans, and Rotis Sans. The end result is a highly legible and stylistically individual typeface that proved to be extremely popular.

The name of the typeface is derived from the area in the town of Leutkirch im Allgäu where Aicher lived.

TRAJAN

ABCDEFGHIJKLM
NOPQRSTUVWXYZ
ABCDEFGHIJKLM
NOPQRSTUVWXYZ
1234567890
(.,:;?!$£&-*){ÀÓÜÇ}

Trajan, based on the lettering inscribed at the base of Trajan's Column in Rome, is one of the earliest typefaces created for Adobe in the late 1980s as part of their expansion into digital type production. Designed by Carol Twombly in 1989, the typeface would go on to become part of Adobe's Modern Ancients Collection of fonts and is one of the best inscribed serifs designed after the shift from hot metal type and photocomposition had occurred. In line with the original Roman inscription Trajan does not contain any lower-case characters, and it has been in constant use by designers ever since, gaining something of a reputation as the default typeface for use on posters promoting movies. The original two-weight family has recently been expanded to include six weights ranging from Extra Light to Black.

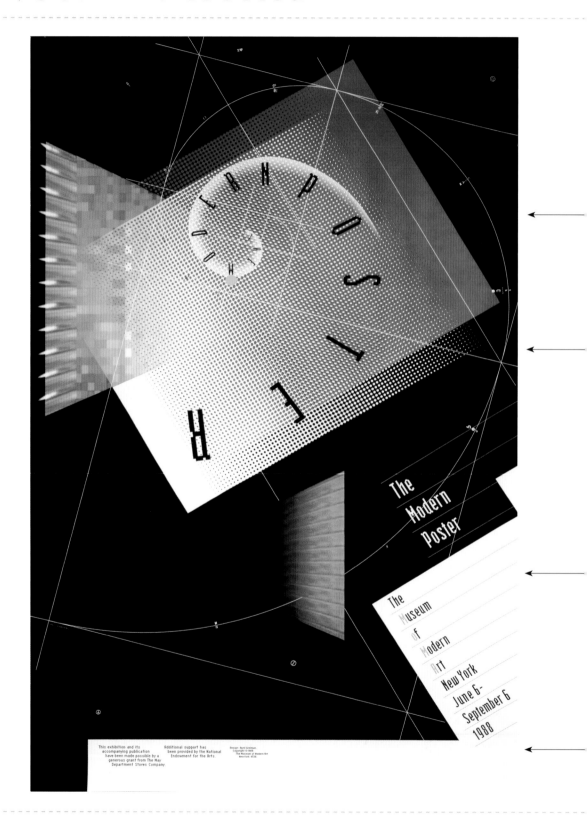

The Modern Poster

April Greiman | 1988

In the early years of digital technology April Greiman began to look for ways in which she could combine digital imagery with analog and hand-drawn elements. Bear in mind that the technology in the 1980s was so new that there were no digital cameras, desktop scanners were very basic, digital printing was extremely limited and so on. Her aim was to try to produce pieces that proclaimed their credentials as graphic design that had been created with digital technology but looked better than simply something that had been "made on a computer." There was a lot of skepticism among members of the design profession around this time and supporters of the new technology much as Greiman had a point to prove, if not to the establishment as a whole then simply to themselves.

The Modern Poster, a five-color offset lithograph created to advertise an exhibition at the Museum of Modern Art in New York, is a great example of combined imagery. There are notes of Greiman's early influences here: the halftone dots and deconstructed nature of the grid are signature features of her previous work, but the elements of colorful video grabs and the 3-D effect created by the overlaid planes were stylistically progressive.

The color palette row below is a sampler of colors selected from the poster shown here, plus some supplementary colors, and is representative of the range of colors a designer working in this style might have used during the 1980s.

Image courtesy of April Greiman

The type set on a curved path and the overlaid geometric diagram introduce movement to the composition and create the impression that the elements are in some way rotating within the frame.

Overlaid planes of color, transparency effects, and halftone dot screens create a very real sense of 3-D despite that fact that all elements sit on the same layer.

Polychrome grids manipulated to create a feeling of extreme perspective are generated from imported video material. Greiman is one of the original pioneers of this technique.

c = 005%	000%	010%	015%	050%	050%	040%	000%
m = 020%	020%	040%	100%	045%	030%	030%	000%
y = 015%	080%	080%	100%	000%	020%	065%	000%
k = 000%	000%	000%	005%	000%	005%	010%	100%

1990s

This decade marks a point in history when multiculturalism, not necessarily a new idea at that time, received a major boost in the shape of the wonderful thing we call the Internet. In egalitarian terms, there had never been anything before it that offered such an accessible method for the dissemination of information. The spread of popular culture across both political and ethnic boundaries required a new graphic language that could be molded easily, adapted quickly, and transmitted efficiently across a wide range of different media platforms.

Fortunately the means to develop this new way of communicating was readily available and digital technology provided graphic designers with the apparatus they needed to make it happen. The decade also marks the point at which the influence of capitalism and a rise in the culture of consumerism would gradually consolidate over the next twenty years to create one of the worst global recessions since the Great Depression of the 1930s.

The opportunities offered by the new technology created overnight entrepreneurs making vast amounts of money before the "dot com" bubble burst and it all came crashing down in 2000, leaving few survivors. This lesson was not lost on an industry which had spent the decade creating an unruly visual brew using a retro-influenced mash-up of styles, and out of it all emerged a brand of graphic designer that in many ways resembled their predecessors from the earlier half of the twentieth century. William Morris would probably have hated the Internet, but his strong moral compass survived and at the century's close graphic design had regained much of its purpose as a means of communicating rather than simply existing as a means to sell more pairs of sneakers.

Above *The cover of the June 1990 issue of
Interview magazine, designed by Fabien Barron
with photography by Herb Ritts.*

The digital age

While the 1990s saw a continued surge in the application of a postmodern approach to graphic design, a penchant for deconstructed typography, and the appropriation of kitsch nostalgic styles, it is probably more important to acknowledge the massive impact that the new technology had on graphic design. The look propagated throughout the 1990s, developing on a constantly climbing curve that followed the development of associated technology, and drew on the visual elements of sci-fi and gaming. Building on a groundwork first set in place by progressive designers such as Wolfgang Weingart and April Greiman, a distinctive digital aesthetic steadily grew. Popular graphic styles continued to retain a deconstructed feel, but the new digital look relied less on the earlier crudeness of heavily bitmapped fonts and low-resolution grunginess, favoring a more polished feel which designers felt reflected the technological advance more effectively.

It is also important to note how software features drove illustration and design styles forward. In 1994 Adobe introduced what is arguably still the most important feature addition in its development history—layers. Prior to this, designers had to work on a single layer in the same way a painter had to work on a single canvas. If you made a mistake, everything beneath it was also destroyed and it was back to the virtual drawing board. With layers everything changed and designers could experiment as much as they wished without risking the work they had already carried out. Illustrations and graphic compositions immediately became more highly detailed and complex after that 1994 release.

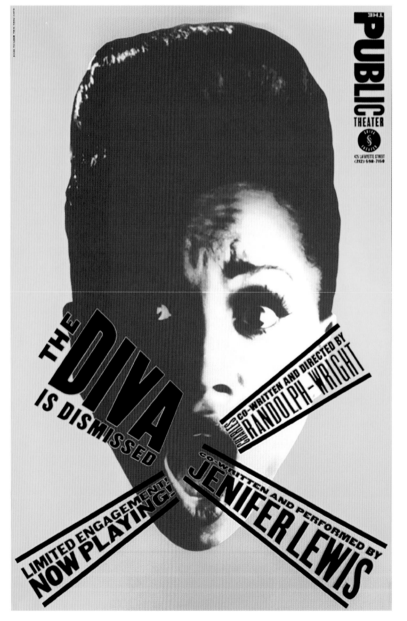

Left *The 1994 poster* The Diva is Dismissed, *designed by Paula Scher for the Public Theatre to advertise an autobiographical show by Jenifer Lewis, draws on the Constructivist style of Russian propaganda posters of the 1920s and 1930s.*
Image courtesy of Pentagram

EMIGRE Nº19:
Starting From
Zero

Price: $7.95

The loss of many of the traditional trades and crafts that once served the graphic design industry represented a downside for the advent of digital technology, with the biggest losers being the typesetting companies. Specialist art workers were able to move sideways by switching their steel rules and X-Acto knives for a mouse and keyboard, but designers eventually took over all typesetting duties. In the early days, the changes presented issues for graphic designers too; years of acquired craftsmanship were swept aside and established design professionals had to acquire new skill sets, not just in the area of typesetting but also in technical areas such as color reproduction and web design techniques. Though a distraction for some during the 1990s, digital design skills are now a part of every graphic designer's toolkit and the issues have vanished. One thing the technology cannot replace is, of course, the development of new concepts and new styles, and the techniques that drive creative problem-solving. These will always remain the responsibility of the designer, and with an ever-expanding set of available tools and experimentation, the development of new graphic design styles has continued apace. However, despite this, graphic designers continue to look back and reference the styles perfected by the generations that came before them.

Above Emigre no. 19, dated 1991, addresses the question "Does experimentation ultimately lead to simplification of graphic design?" and is set entirely in Template Gothic, a font designed by Cranbrook student Barry Deck (see page 214).
Image courtesy of Emigre

Left Emigre no. 49, dated 1999, was built editorially around the original First Things First Manifesto (see page 205).
Image courtesy of Emigre

1990s

The resurgence of the handmade

The saying "What goes around comes around" is as applicable to graphic design as it is to any other walk of life, and by the end of the twentieth century many designers were experimenting enthusiastically with methods which would allow them to combine the new digital technology with older "handmade" techniques. A feeling that graphic design style was becoming homogenized by technology and was lacking in concept manifested itself during the 1990s, and justifiably so. Styles were often driven by significant new software features that were introduced; when Shadowcaster, a very effective but initially overused extension for QuarkXPress, was developed by A Lowly Apprentice Production in the early 1990s, drop shadows became ubiquitous for months on end before the novelty eventually wore off.

However, despite all this, graphic design has managed to continue to steer an aesthetic path which embraces both new technology and old techniques. In those terms, the biggest challenge for graphic designers today is, as ever, to resist the temptation to allow the technology to define the idea. At the end of the day graphic design is still about clear, effective, and when appropriate stylish communication, and it is for designers themselves to continue this process rather than the machines in front of them which are still only tools that should and must be used wisely.

Above The poster for Lou Reed's album Set the Twilight Reeling was designed by Stefan Sagmeister in 1996 using a technique intended to connect the artist directly to his lyrics using a faux tattoo effect with hand-drawn typography.

Right Despite Max Kisman's early adoption of digital technology, this 2001 exhibition poster demonstrates the wonderful sense of joie de vivre associated with Toulouse-Lautrec by utilizing a distinctly "un-digital" visual style and hand-drawn typography.

First Things First Manifesto 2000

Written in the Fall of 1999 and published simultaneously in *Adbusters*, *Emigre (Issue no. 51)*, *AIGA Journal of Graphic Design*, *Eye magazine* issue no. 33 vol. 8, *Blueprint*, and *Items*, the *First Things First Manifesto 2000* is an updated version of the original manifesto written by British designer and activist Ken Garland (see page 141) in 1964. As before, the text received a mixed reception from the industry but achieved its aim of reopening the debate on what the true priorities of graphic design as a profession should be. It seems fitting to end the narrative section of this book by reproducing a statement which challenges today's graphic designers to look carefully at their own practices, and perhaps to reflect on the vast body of work created during the twentieth century, in order to remind themselves of the sense of responsibility and moral obligation that has informed the work of so many graphic designers before them.

We, the undersigned, are graphic designers, art directors and visual communicators who have been raised in a world in which the techniques and apparatus of advertising have persistently been presented to us as the most lucrative, effective and desirable use of our talents. Many design teachers and mentors promote this belief; the market rewards it; a tide of books and publications reinforces it.

Encouraged in this direction, designers then apply their skill and imagination to sell dog biscuits, designer coffee, diamonds, detergents, hair gel, cigarettes, credit cards, sneakers, butt toners, light beer and heavy-duty recreational vehicles. Commercial work has always paid the bills, but many graphic designers have now let it become, in large measure, what graphic designers do. This, in turn, is how the world perceives design. The profession's time and energy is used up manufacturing demand for things that are inessential at best.

Many of us have grown increasingly uncomfortable with this view of design. Designers who devote their efforts primarily to advertising, marketing and brand development are supporting, and implicitly endorsing, a mental environment so saturated with commercial messages that it is changing the very way citizen-consumers speak, think, feel, respond and interact. To some extent we are all helping draft a reductive and immeasurably harmful code of public discourse.

There are pursuits more worthy of our problem-solving skills. Unprecedented environmental, social and cultural crises demand our attention. Many cultural interventions, social marketing campaigns, books, magazines, exhibitions, educational tools, television programmes, films, charitable causes and other information design projects urgently require our expertise and help.

We propose a reversal of priorities in favour of more useful, lasting and democratic forms of communication – a mindshift away from product marketing and toward the exploration and production of a new kind of meaning. The scope of debate is shrinking; it must expand. Consumerism is running uncontested; it must be challenged by other perspectives expressed, in part, through the visual languages and resources of design.

In 1964, 22 visual communicators signed the original call for our skills to be put to worthwhile use. With the explosive growth of global commercial culture, their message has only grown more urgent. Today, we renew their manifesto in expectation that no more decades will pass before it is taken to heart.

The manifesto was signed by thirty-three prominent members of the design community; Jonathan Barnbrook, Nick Bell, Andrew Blauvelt, Hans Bockting, Irma Boom, Sheila Levrant de Bretteville, Max Bruinsma, Siân Cook, Linda van Deursen, Chris Dixon, William Drenttel, Gert Dumbar, Simon Esterson, Vince Frost, Ken Garland, Milton Glaser, Jessica Helfand, Steven Heller, Andrew Howard, Tibor Kalman, Jeffery Keedy, Zuzana Licko, Ellen Lupton, Katherine McCoy, Armand Mevis, J. Abbott Miller, Rick Poynor, Lucienne Roberts, Erik Spiekermann, Jan van Toorn, Teal Triggs, Rudy VanderLans, and Bob Wilkinson.

Tibor Kalman

Tibor Kalman was born in Budapest in 1949 and emigrated to the U.S. in 1956 when his family fled the Soviet invasion of Hungary, settling in New York. He first studied journalism at New York University in 1968, becoming an organizer for SDS (Students for a Democratic Society), but dropped out after a year and went to work at the bookstore which would eventually grow into the large Barnes & Noble chain. He was responsible for the store's publicity and commissioned graphic designers, from whom he began to learn about the design trade, and, in time, he became the manager of the store's in-house design department.

Above *Humor played a large part in Kalman's posters for Restaurant Florent, circa 1987. The quality of the typography is secondary to the concept, which mocks the slicker style of competing advertising material.*

By 1979 he decided he was ready for a creative career of his own, and moved to establish M&Co, a firm he cofounded with Carol Bokuniewicz and Liz Trovato.

The studio quickly achieved success through a list of prestigious and fashionable clients, including the band Talking Heads and the New-York based journal *Art Forum*. Other clients included the fashion retailer Limited Brands (now L Brands Inc.) and the much-loved institution Restaurant Florent located in New York's Meatpacking District. Florent Morellet needed a designer who could create something atypical of the generic styling applied to other restaurants and appreciated Kalman's knowledge and application of the American vernacular in his work. By the early 1990s Kalman was also working as the creative director for *Interview* magazine.

Aside from his design work, the interesting thing about Kalman was how he influenced other designers to think in terms of their place in the world—their role toward society and toward the furtherance of design culture. He was by turns a fiercely moral person who would often denounce what he felt was exploitative or unethical, and an arch-provocateur who would happily create pieces designed to shock in order to extract a strong reaction. Never afraid to go one further to get his point across, Kalman was often referred to as the "bad boy" of graphic design.

His work for *Interview* came to the attention of Oliviero Toscani, the advertising director for the international clothing chain Benetton, and in 1990 Kalman was asked to create a proposal for a magazine which would be published by the company. The content of *Colors* focused on multiculturalism and global awareness, and like the preceding "United Colors of Benetton" advertising campaign the content was often controversial. A prime example of the way Kalman used imagery to provoke reaction is the article about racial prejudice titled "What If...?" which appeared in issue no. 4, published in 1992. Using doctored portraits it depicts Pope John Paul II as Asian, Spike Lee and Michael Jackson (oddly

prophetic as it turns out) as white, and Arnold Schwarzenegger and Queen Elizabeth II as black. Kalman had been made editor-in-chief of *Colors* in 1991, and by 1993 he decided to close the doors at M&Co and move to Rome in order to work solely on the magazine. Three years later he was diagnosed with non-Hodgkins lymphoma which forced a decision to return to New York where, despite undergoing a debilitating treatment regime, he reopened M&Co and continued to work on projects for which he felt a strong empathy. Kalman died in Puerto Rico in 1999, shortly before a retrospective of his graphic design work entitled "Tiborocity" began its U.S. tour at the San Francisco Museum of Modern Art.

Left and below *The cover and a spread from* Race, *issue no. 4 of* Colors *magazine.*
Courtesy of Colors Magazine

what if..?
e se..?

David Carson

David Carson is a graphic designer, a teacher, and a surfer—the surfer part is as important as it indicates an outlook on life which comes through in the work of the "Paganini of Type," a nickname of Carson's attributed to graphic designer Jeffrey Keedy. Carson was born in Texas in 1956 and graduated from San Diego State University with a BA in Sociology, going on to become a lecturer in higher education and a professional surfer, achieving a top ten world ranking in 1989.

He received little formal training in graphic design, but an interest was sparked by a brief design workshop he attended in Switzerland. Carson continued to experiment with graphic design and typography, and his first experience of professional art direction came when he began working on the re-styling of *Transworld Skateboarding* (*TWS*) in 1984. The assignment was perfect for Carson as his background as a surfer meant he was completely au fait with the content, and

the kind of magazine *TWS* aspired to be meant he was able to experiment fully with the design style, eschewing conventional layout restraints. It was during his tenure at *TWS* that he developed his signature style of typography which would become known as "grunge" type.

By 1989 he had been asked by Steve and Debbee Pezman, the publishers of *Surfer* magazine, to design and art-direct the quarterly magazine *Beach Culture* which had started life as a trade publication. The large-format magazine ran for just six issues but Carson's radical approach to the design and typography, often featuring layouts that paid little regard to the rules of legibility and readability, had by this time caught the attention of the graphic design world. Many designers were dismissive of his grungy style and considered it to be ill-conceived and amateurish, but nobody cared to deny how innovative

Above *A selection of early* Ray Gun *covers.*

and influential it was. His approach was essentially to deconstruct the typography by rejecting the Modernist ideal of "form follows function" in favor of a method where the type and layout expresses itself literally through its form. There are clear parallels to be drawn between Carson's style and Dada (see page 47), once again illustrating the predilection for Postmodernism to borrow ideas from historical design styles.

Carson worked on *Beach Culture* from 1989 to 1991 before taking on the design of *Surfer* from 1991 to 1993, where he continued to create layouts in his distinctive and offbeat style. However, the project for which he is arguably best known began in 1992 when publisher Marvin Scott Jarrett hired Carson to create a new music and lifestyle magazine by the name of *Ray Gun*. Working on the magazine for the next three years, Carson was able to refine (if that word could possibly be applied to his work during this period!) his approach to type and layout to its limit. His most infamous layout is arguably the 1994 Bryan Ferry interview which he reportedly found so dull he set the text in Zapf Dingbats, although, to be fair, the text was reproduced in readable form later in the magazine.

In 1995 Carson founded his own studio, David Carson Design, in New York, where his stellar client list came to include Nike, Microsoft, Giorgio Armani, Pepsi Cola, Levi Strauss, and American Airlines, to name but a few. His cover design for the first issue of travel magazine *Blue* (1997) was named among the top forty best magazine covers of all time by the American Society of Magazine Editors. He continues to work on numerous projects and lectures extensively around the world.

Modern Dog

During the mid- to late-1980s, a lot of tan- or gray-colored boxes began to appear on graphic designer's desks. This was a good thing in so many ways and we all have them, except now they are better-looking, silver, and less boxy. Unfortunately, for a while Apple Macintosh computers did cause graphic design to polarize and a lot of work began to look quite similar, as did whatever could be created during the early years of desktop publishing. Fortunately, Robynne Raye and Michael Strassburger of Modern Dog chose to plough their own furrow and ignored what most other designers were doing. They stuck to what they liked, and effectively are still following the same philosophy today, creating work that is fresh in a Dada-meets-Psychedelia-meets-Punk meets Modern Dog kind of way.

Raye and Strassburger met at Western Washington University while both studying graphic design and working at the college radio station. After graduation in 1986 they pursued separate career paths; Raye worked as a production designer while Strassburger was employed at an exhibition design company. However, difficulties in finding alternative work as graphic designers prompted them to pool their resources and seek freelance commissions, primarily in the form of theater posters as a response to the flourishing scene in Seattle. Success prompted the decision to form a company, and for two weeks they were Raye Strassburger Design. Citing this as sounding too much like a law firm, the name quickly changed to Modern Dog after Strassburger commented on a "modern dog" drawn on a sign for a grooming parlor. Raye immediately suggested they call the company Modern Dog, and that was that.

They are well known for their poster designs, acknowledged by the book *Modern Dog: 20 Years of Poster Art* published by Chronicle in 2008. The styles of execution across their considerable body of work are many and varied but one common thread running through a large portion of it is their undeniable sense of humor. Other work categories include books, brochures, clothing, corporate identity, packaging, and product design. The K2 corporation, an American ski and snowboarding company, was an important client during the 1990s, and Modern Dog designed a series of brochures featuring covers influenced by Herbert Matter's Swiss Tourism posters from the 1930s (see page 96-97). Another long-standing relationship, with Mitch Nash at Blue Q, has produced a range of products including the Cat Butt fridge magnets and Sparkling Mullet body and car wash.

Their extensive client list includes advertising agencies Ogilvy and Mather and TBWA/Chiat/Day; most of the major record labels and many independents; the AIGA and Icograda; Levi Strauss, Hasbro; the *New York Times*; Adidas and Nike; Adobe and Microsoft, to name a few. Raye and Strassburger are also both lecturers at Cornish College of Arts in Seattle.

Modern Dog can be seen to represent the acme of Postmodernism, drawing on design styles which range from the beginning of the twentieth century to the present day. Perhaps more importantly, while they take their work and their company very seriously, they provide us with an example of how it is possible not to take graphic design itself too seriously. A lot has been written about the strictness of rules and the formality of good typography over the years, but one does not necessarily have to follow the rules to create great graphic design.

Opposite *Influenced by 1920s Russian Constructivist style, the 1992 poster for the Flying Karamazov Brothers featured moving arms and eyes that swivelled back and forth.* **Courtesy of Modern Dog**

Top right *Work for the K2 Corporation, a ski and snowboarding company based in Washington State, made up a large portion of Modern Dog's workload during the 1990s with commissions ranging from product catalogs to actual deck designs.* **Courtesy of Modern Dog**

Right *Modern Dog have designed numerous posters for the Greenwood Arts Council's Artwalk, each of which features a character illustrated in a different artistic style. This example dates from 1998.* **Courtesy of Modern Dog**

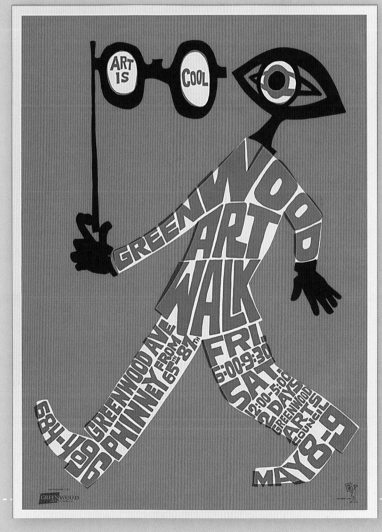

Dax

PMN

*

Interstate

Template

Gothic *

Meta

Mrs Eaves

Caecilia
Scala
DIN
Filosofia
Giza

By the 1990s, major improvements in digital print technology had begun to emerge and type designers began once again to look at broader points of reference to inform their work on new typeface design. The decade marks the beginnings of the modern digital type foundry, and new faces influenced by any number of historical references were published during the 1990s. The enormous level of output continues to the present day.

FF Scala
Martin Majoor | 1990–98

Template Gothic
Barry Deck | 1989–91

PMN Caecilia
Peter Matthias Noordzij | 1991

FF Meta
Erik Spiekermann | 1991–2003

Interstate
Tobias Frere-Jones | 1993–99

Giza
David Berlow | 1994

FF DIN
Albert-Jan Pool | 1994–2001

FF Dax
Hans Reichel | 1995–2003

Filosofia
Zuzana Licko | 1996

Mrs Eaves
Zuzana Licko | 1996

Template Gothic

ABCDEFGHIJKLM
NOPQRSTUVWXYZ
abcdefghijklm
nopqrstuvwxyz
1234567890
(.,:;?!$£&-*){ÀÓÜÇ}

Template Gothic defines the look of 1990s typography perfectly as a time when many experimental typefaces were created. It was designed by Barry Deck in 1989 while he was still a student at the California Institute of the Arts and was released commercially by type foundry and publisher Emigre in 1991. Cofounder Rudy VanderLans was shown the typeface during a class visit to the Emigre studio and liked what he saw. Deck's inspiration came from a hand-lettered sign he spotted at his local laundromat which featured characters applied (quite badly) with a template. He loved the imperfections of the character shapes and decided to create a typeface which would reflect the organic nature of the letterforms and connect with the distorted typeface styles from the photocomposition era.

Interstate

ABCDEFGHIJKLM
NOPQRSTUVWXYZ
abcdefghijklm
nopqrstuvwxyz
1234567890
(.,:;?!$£&-*){ÀÓÜÇ}

Interstate, a geometric sans-serif, was created by the well-known typeface designer Tobias Frere-Jones between 1993 and 1999 and closely interprets the collection of fonts known as the FHWA series, created by the Federal Highway Administration in 1949 for use on signage throughout the road network in the US. Frere-Jones's typeface is far more than simply a signage and display font and features many refinements that allow it to be used successfully as a text font in both print and web environments. For a geometric sans-serif it has a very approachable feel and is highly legible in all point sizes. The complete Interstate family stretches to forty styles with weights ranging from hairline to ultra black, and it includes both condensed and compressed versions.

DIN

ABCDEFGHIJKLM
NOPQRSTUVWXYZ
abcdefghijklm
nopqrstuvwxyz
1234567890
(.,:;?!$£&-*){ÀÓÜÇ}

The story of DIN starts way back in the 1930s with DIN 1451 when it was designed at the *Deutsches Institut für Normung* (DIN), which translates as the German Institute for Standardization. The typeface was created to provide a standard font that could be used on everything from signage to technical drawings and subsequently—in all its various releases over the years—it has a very precise, engineered look to it. It has been used ever since on practically all public signage throughout Germany and broke through into mainstream use in the 1990s when it was released by Adobe and Linotype as DIN Mittelschrift. In 1994 Albert-Jan Pool expanded the character set for FF DIN, released through FontFont, and subsequent additions to the range of styles have created a superfamily of highly functional typefaces.

Mrs Eaves

ABCDEFGHIJKLM
NOPQRSTUVWXYZ
abcdefghijklm
nopqrstuvwxyz
1234567890
(.,:;?!$£&-*){ÀÓÜÇ}

Mrs Eaves was designed by Zuzana Licko of Emigre in 1996. The letterforms are based on her interpretation of the all-time classic Baskerville, an ever-popular serif typeface designed and cut in the 1750s. Up to that point Licko was better known for her radical typefaces designed during the 1980s when Apple Macs first arrived on the scene, but Mrs Eaves was a very different proposition. Designed primarily as a typeface suited to body text, the letterforms distance themselves from the relative severity of Baskerville and take on a softer look which is extremely characterful. The x-height is fairly small and the serifs noticeably prominent, giving text set in Mrs Eaves a slightly hunkered-down look. It is named after Sarah Rushton Eaves, who was John Baskerville's housekeeper, and later his wife.

Black type on a yellow background provides extremely high contrast and helps preserve the legibility of the typography in this busy poster layout.

Symbols attached to each separate performance detailed on the poster indicate which part of the theater is hosting the event.

Space is not wasted by adding complex information against each separate performance. The message is maximized using the large punchy typography and a prominent phone number is listed in two different places on the layout, encouraging people to call for details.

Black and white photography applied as a photomontage is reminiscent of Russian Constructivism, a style which enjoyed a resurgence in popularity during the 1990s.

Bring in 'da Noise, Bring in 'da Funk

Paula Scher | 1995

When the Public Theater in New York City began to experience dwindling box-office returns and a reduction in membership fees, the theatre's newly appointed director, George C. Wolfe, approached Paula Scher for help. He wanted to draw in a younger, more vibrant audience that could transform the demographic of a typical Public Theater audience into one that was culturally aware and more switched on to current trends in music and performance.

Scher's answer was to take her influence from the bold statement style of 1800s American wood-type posters, creating illustrative word clouds with the details of each performance in bold type set both vertically and horizontally, and at angles which cut into each other to create dynamic relationships between negative and positive space. By rejecting the standard form of theater poster, she created pieces that stood out from other promotional material posted around the City.

Arguably the best example from the mid-1990s is the poster shown here, designed to promote the street-tap musical Bring in 'da Noise, Bring in 'da Funk. The immensely appealing style propagated across all forms of printed media and became one of the most imitated graphic design styles of the late 1990s.

The color palette row below is a sampler of colors selected from the poster shown here, plus some supplementary colors, and is representative of the range of colors a designer working in this style might have used during the 1990s.

Image courtesy of Pentagram

c =	005%	000%	000%	005%	090%	085%	040%	000%
m =	000%	030%	090%	100%	010%	085%	030%	000%
y =	100%	100%	080%	100%	000%	000%	030%	000%
k =	000%	000%	000%	000%	000%	000%	010%	100%

Selected bibliography

In print

• *20th Century Type*, Lewis Blackwell
• *The Anatomy of Type*, Stephen Coles
• *The Anatomy of Design, Uncovering the Influences and Inspirations in Modern Graphic Design*, Steven Heller and Mirko Ilić
• *An A-Z of Type Designers*, Neil Macmillan
• *British Prints from the Machine Age, Rhythms of Modern Life*, Clifford S. Ackley
• *Dutch Graphic Design, A Century of Innovation*, Alston W. Purvis and Cees W. de Jong
• *E. McKnight Kauffer*, Brian Webb and Peyton Skipwith
• *Front Cover, Great Book Jacket and Cover Design*, Alan Powers
• *Graphic Design, A History*, Stephen J. Eskilson
• *The Graphic Language of Neville Brody*, Jon Wozencroft
• *Graphic Design Timeline, A Century of Design Milestones*, Steven Heller and Elinor Pettit
• *Meggs' History of Graphic Design, Fifth Edition*, Philip B. Meggs and Alston W. Purvis
• *Modern Dog, 20 Years of Poster Art*, Mike Strassburger and Robynne Raye
• *The Phaidon Archive of Graphic Design*
• *Saul Bass*, Jennifer Bass and Pat Kirkham
• *Stenberg Brothers, Constructing a Revolution in Soviet Design*, Christopher Mount
• *The Wonderground Map of London Town*, Geoffrey Kichenside
• *Typography Now, The Next Wave*, Rick Poynor

Online

• *AIGA*, http://www.aiga.org
• *A. M. Cassandre*, www.cassandre-france.com
• *Alvin Lustig*, www.alvinlustig.com
• *The Art of Poster*, theartofposter.com
• *Art of the Poster 1880-1980 (MCAD Library)* www.flickr.com/photos/69184488@N06/sets/72157636362161535/
• *Beinecke Rare Book and Manuscript Library*, beinecke.library.yale.edu
• *The Cranbrook Archives*, www.cranbrook.edu/center/archives
• *Emigre Magazine*, www.emigre.com
• *Eye Magazine*, www.eyemagazine.com
• *Graphic Design Archive (RIT Libraries)*, library.rit.edu/gda/
• *The Herb Lubalin Study Center of Design and Typography*, lubalincenter.cooper.edu
• *Herbert Matter*, herbertmatter.org
• *Herman Miller Inc.*, www.hermanmiller.com/why/irving-harper-the-mediums-beyond-the-message.html
• *The Merrill C. Berman Collection*, mcbcollection.com
• *Monotype: Pencil to Pixel*, recorder.monotype.com/pencil-to-pixel/
• *Paul Rand*, www.paul-rand.com
• *The Red List*, theredlist.com
• *The Saul Bass Poster Archive*, www.saulbassposterarchive.com
• *Typographische Monatsblätter*, www.tm-research-archive.ch

Image credits

All images in this book are public domain unless otherwise stated.

Every effort has been made to credit the copyright holders of the images used in this book. We apologize for any unintentional omissions or errors and will insert the appropriate acknowledgement to any companies or individuals in subsequent editions of the work.

Index

Acknowledgements

The success of this book relies in part on the imagery that we were able to source in support of the text, and I am extremely grateful to everyone that took the time to help us with our legion requests. In particular I would like to thank Merrill C. Berman and Joelle Jensen at the Merrill C. Berman Collection; Allan Kohl and the Minneapolis College of Art and Design; Herman Miller; Ken Garland; Lance Wyman; Alexander Tochilovsky and The Herb Lubalin Study Center of Design and Typography; John Pasche; Allan Haley and Monotype; Paula Scher and Pentagram; Hearst Magazines; *i-D* magazine; Caitlin Wunderlich and the Cranbrook Academy of Art; Dodo van Aarem and Studio Dumbar; April Greiman; Rudy VanderLans and Emigre; Sagmeister & Walsh; Max Kisman, Mauro Bedoni and *Colors* magazine; and Robynne Raye at Modern Dog. If I've missed anyone from the list, please accept my apologies.

I'd also like thank the team at Quid Publishing; James Evans for proposing we put together the concept for this book and for his customary level of support throughout the project, Nigel Browning for giving the project the green light, and Dee Costello who contributed so much to the editorial and picture research tasks. It has once again been a pleasure to work with them.

Finally, to my family and friends who are always there to give me a boost when the impetus begins to flag, and to my wife Sarah for her endless encouragement and patient support, you have my gratitude.

In memory of Patricia Keith, 1939–2013.